THE CIRCLE

A Comedy in Three Acts

by

W. SOMERSET MAUGHAM

SAMUEL   FRENCH

LONDON

NEW YORK TORONTO SYDNEY HOLLYWOOD

THE CIRCLE

First produced at the Haymarket Theatre, London, on 3rd March, 1921, with the following cast of characters :—

(In order of their appearance.)

ARNOLD CHAMPION-CHENEY, M.P. . .	*Ernest Thesiger*
FOOTMAN	*Cecil Trouncer*
MRS. SHENSTONE.	*Tonie Edgar-Bruce*
ELIZABETH	*Fay Compton*
EDWARD LUTON	*Leon Quartermaine*
CLIVE CHAMPION-CHENEY . . .	*E. Holman Clark*
BUTLER	*W. W. Palmer*
LADY CATHERINE CHAMPION-CHENEY .	*Lottie Venne*
LORD PORTEOUS	*Allan Aynesworth*

The Play was revived at the Vaudeville Theatre, London, on 26th February, 1931, with the following cast of characters :—

ARNOLD CHAMPION-CHENEY, M.P. . .	*Frank Vosper*
FOOTMAN	*Noel Cortland*
MRS. SHENSTONE.	*Violet Campbell*
ELIZABETH	*Celia Johnson*
EDWARD LUTON	*Peter Hannen*
CLIVE CHAMPION-CHENEY . . .	*Nigel Playfair*
BUTLER	*Brian Powley*
LADY CATHERINE CHAMPION-CHENEY .	*Athene Seyler*
LORD PORTEOUS	*Allan Aynesworth*

The play produced by RAYMOND MASSEY

The Play was again revived at the Haymarket Theatre, London, on 11th October, 1945, with the following cast of characters :—

ARNOLD CHAMPION-CHENEY, M.P. . .	*John Gielgud*
FOOTMAN	*John Blatchley*
MRS. SHENSTONE.	*Dorothy Lane*
ELIZABETH	*Rosalie Crutchley*
EDWARD LUTON	*Patrick Crean*
CLIVE CHAMPION-CHENEY . . .	*Cecil Trouncer*
BUTLER	*Francis Drake*
LADY CATHERINE CHAMPION-CHENEY .	*Yvonne Arnaud*
LORD PORTEOUS	*Leslie Banks*

The play produced by WILLIAM ARMSTRONG

———

SYNOPSIS OF SCENES

The action of the play takes place in the drawing-room at Aston-Adey, Arnold Champion-Cheney's house in Dorset.

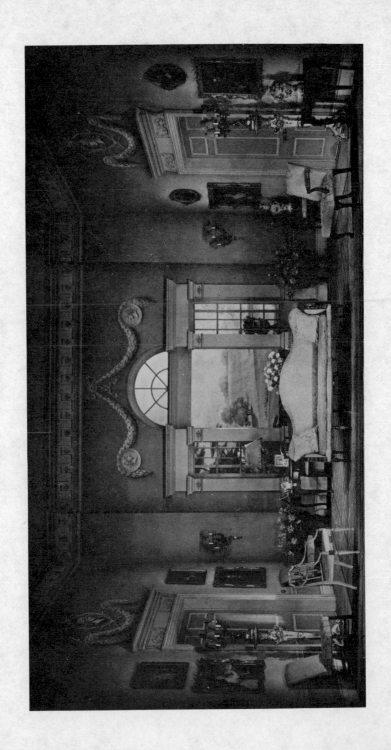

THE CIRCLE

ACT I

The Scene is a stately drawing-room at Aston-Adey, with fine pictures on the walls and Georgian furniture. (See the Ground Plan, Photograph, and Furniture Plots.) Aston-Adey has been described, with many illustrations, in Country Life. *It is not a house, but a place. Its owner takes a great pride in it, and there is nothing in the room which is not of the period. Through the french windows at the back can be seen the beautiful gardens which are one of the features.*

It is a fine summer morning.

ARNOLD *enters* L. *He is a man of about thirty-five, tall and good-looking, fair, with a clean-cut, sensitive face. He has a look which is intellectual, but somewhat bloodless. He is very well dressed.*

ARNOLD (*calling*). Elizabeth ! (*He goes to the window and calls again.*) Elizabeth ! (*He crosses* R. *and rings the bell. While he is waiting he gives a look round the room. He slightly alters the position of the chair* R. *of the settee.*)

(*A* FOOTMAN *enters* L.)

Oh, George ! See if you can find Mrs. Cheney, and ask her if she'd be good enough to come here.

FOOTMAN. Very good, sir.

(*The* FOOTMAN *turns to go.*)

ARNOLD (*crossing* L. *above the settee*). Who is supposed to look after this room ?

FOOTMAN. I don't know, sir.

ARNOLD (*adjusting the vase on the table up* L.). I wish when they dust they'd take care to replace the things exactly as they were before.

FOOTMAN. Yes, sir.

ARNOLD (*dismissing him*). All right.

(*The* FOOTMAN *exits* L.)

(ARNOLD *crosses* R. *to the dining-room doors, opens them, and calls.*)

ARNOLD. Elizabeth !

(ANNA SHENSTONE *enters from the garden. She is a woman of forty, pleasant and of elegant appearance.* ARNOLD *turns and sees her.*)

Oh, Anna, do you know where Elizabeth is ?

5

ANNA. I think she's gone up to change. She's been playing tennis with Mr. Luton.

ARNOLD. Something very tiresome has happened. (*He moves* R.C.)

ANNA (*moving down* L.). Oh ?

ARNOLD. I wonder where the deuce she is.

ANNA (*moving to below the settee*). When d'you expect Lord Porteous and Lady Kitty ?

ARNOLD. They're motoring down in time for luncheon.

ANNA. Are you sure you want me here ? It's not too late yet, you know. I can have my things packed and catch a train for somewhere or other.

ARNOLD. No, of course we want you. It'll make it so much easier if there are people here. It was exceedingly kind of you to come.

ANNA (*moving to the* L. *end of the settee*). Oh, nonsense ! (*She sits.*)

ARNOLD (R. *of the settee*). And I think it was a good thing to have Teddie Luton down.

ANNA. He is so breezy, isn't he ?

ARNOLD. Yes, that's his great asset. I don't know that he's very intelligent, but, you know, there are occasions when you want a bull in a china shop. (*Moving up to* C.) I sent one of the servants to find Elizabeth. Really it can't take all this time to change one's dress. (*He moves back to below* R. *of the settee.*)

ANNA (*with a smile*). One can't change one's dress without powdering one's nose, you know.

(ELIZABETH *enters* L. *She is a very pretty creature in the early twenties. She wears a light summer frock.*)

ARNOLD. My dear, I've been hunting for you everywhere. What *have* you been doing ?

ELIZABETH (*closing the door*). Nothing ! (*Moving to the chair* L. *of the settee.*) I've been standing on my head.

ARNOLD. My father's here.

ELIZABETH (*startled*). Where ?

ARNOLD. At the cottage. He arrived last night.

ELIZABETH. Damn ! (*She sits on the upper arm of the chair.*)

ARNOLD (*good-humouredly*). I wish you wouldn't say that, Elizabeth. (*He waves her off the arm of the chair.*)

ELIZABETH (*rising*). If you're not going to say " Damn " when a thing's damnable, when are you going to say " Damn " ? (*She sits in the chair* L.)

ARNOLD. I should have thought you could say, " Oh, bother ! " or something like that.

ELIZABETH. But that wouldn't express my sentiments. Besides, at that speech day when you were giving away the prizes you said there were no synonyms in the English language.

ANNA (*smiling*). Oh, Elizabeth ! It's very unfair to expect a politician to live in private up to the statements he makes in public.

ARNOLD. I'm always willing to stand by anything I've said. There *are* no synonyms in the English language.

ELIZABETH. In that case I shall be regretfully forced to continue to say " Damn " whenever I feel like it.

ARNOLD. I . . .

(EDWARD LUTON *shows himself at the window. He is an attractive youth in flannels.* ARNOLD *moves up.*)

TEDDIE (*at the window*). I say, Elizabeth, what about another single ? Oh, you've changed.

ELIZABETH. Come in. We're having a scene.

TEDDIE (*moving down* L.C.). How splendid ! What about ?

ELIZABETH. The English language.

TEDDIE. Don't tell me you've been splitting your infinitives.

ARNOLD (*at* R., *with the shadow of a frown*). I wish you'd be serious, Elizabeth. The situation is none too pleasant.

ANNA. I think Teddie and I had better make ourselves scarce.

ELIZABETH (*rising*). Nonsense ! (*Crossing to down* C., *sitting* L. *of* ANNA). You're both in it. If there's going to be any unpleasantness we want your moral support. That's why we asked you to come.

TEDDIE. And I thought I'd been asked for my blue eyes.

ELIZABETH. Vain beast ! And they happen to be brown.

TEDDIE (*above the chair* L.). Is anything up ? (*He sits on the arm of the chair.*)

ELIZABETH. Arnold's father arrived last night.

TEDDIE. Did he, by Jove ! (*To* ARNOLD.) I thought he was in Paris.

ARNOLD. So did we all. He told me he'd be there for the next month.

ANNA. Have you seen him ?

ARNOLD. No, he rang me up. It's a mercy he had a telephone put in the cottage. It would have been a pretty kettle of fish if he'd just walked in.

ELIZABETH. Did you tell him Lady Catherine was coming ?

ARNOLD. Of course not. (R. *of the settee.*) I was flabbergasted to know he was here. And then I thought we'd better talk it over first.

ELIZABETH. Is he coming along here ?

ARNOLD. Yes. He suggested it, and I couldn't think of any excuse to prevent him.

TEDDIE. Couldn't you put the other people off ?

ARNOLD. They're coming by car.

(TEDDIE *sits in the chair* L.)

They may be here any minute. It's too late to do that.

ELIZABETH. Besides, it would be beastly.

ARNOLD. I knew it was silly to have them here. Elizabeth
insisted.

ELIZABETH. After all, she *is* your mother, Arnold.

ARNOLD. That meant precious little to her when she — went
away. You can't imagine it means very much to me now.

ELIZABETH. It's thirty years ago. It seems so absurd to bear
malice after all that time.

ARNOLD. I don't bear malice, but the fact remains that she did
me the most irreparable harm. I can find no excuse for her.

ELIZABETH. Have you ever tried to ?

ARNOLD. My dear Elizabeth, it's no good going over all that
again. The facts are lamentably simple. She had a husband who
adored her, a wonderful position, all the money she could want,
and a child of five. And she ran away with a married man.

ELIZABETH. Lady Porteous is not a very attractive woman,
Arnold. (*To* ANNA.) Do you know her ?

ANNA (*smiling*). " Forbidding " is the word, I think.

ARNOLD. If you're going to make little jokes about it, I have
nothing more to say. (*He sits in the chair* R.)

ANNA. I'm sorry, Arnold.

(*A slight pause.*)

ELIZABETH. Perhaps your mother couldn't help herself — if she
was in love ?

(TEDDIE *glances at* ELIZABETH.)

ARNOLD. And had no sense of honour, duty, or decency ?
Oh, yes, under those circumstances you can explain a great deal.

ELIZABETH. That's not a very pretty way to speak of your
mother.

ARNOLD. I can't look on her as my mother.

ELIZABETH. What you can't get over is that she didn't think of
you. Some of us are more mother and some of us more woman.
It gives me a little thrill when I think that she loved that man so
much. She sacrificed her name, her position, and her child to him.

ARNOLD. You really can't expect the said child to have any
great affection for the mother who treated him like that.

ELIZABETH. No, I don't think I do. But I think it's a pity after
all these years that you shouldn't be friends.

ARNOLD (*as he rises*). I wonder if you realise what it was to
grow up under the shadow of that horrible scandal. Everywhere,
at school, and at Oxford, and afterwards in London, I was always
the son of Lady Kitty Cheney. Oh, it was cruel, cruel ! (*He moves
a little up stage.*)

ELIZABETH. Yes, I know, Arnold. It was beastly for you.

ARNOLD. It would have been bad enough if it had been an
ordinary case, but the position of the people made it ten times
worse. (*He moves down a little.*) My father was in the House then,

and Porteous — he hadn't succeeded to the title — was in the House too ; he was Under-Secretary for Foreign Affairs, and he was very much in the public eye.

ANNA.   My father always used to say he was the ablest man in the party. Every one was expecting him to be Prime Minister.

ARNOLD.   You can imagine what a boon it was to the British public. They hadn't had such a treat for a generation. The most popular song of the day was about my mother. Did you ever hear it ? (*Crossing above the settee to* L.) " Naughty Lady Kitty. Thought it such a pity . . . "

ELIZABETH (*interrupting*). Oh, Arnold, don't !

ARNOLD.   And then they never let people forget them. If they'd lived quietly in Florence and not made a fuss the scandal would have died down. (*Crossing back to above the chair* R.) But those constant actions between Lord and Lady Porteous kept on reminding everyone.

TEDDIE.   What were they having actions about ?

ARNOLD.   Of course my father divorced his wife, but Lady Porteous refused to divorce Porteous. He tried to force her by refusing to support her and turning her out of her house, and heaven knows what. They were constantly wrangling in the law courts.

ANNA.   I think it was monstrous of Lady Porteous.

ARNOLD.   She knew that Porteous wanted to marry my mother, and she hated my mother. You can't blame her.

ANNA.   It must have been very difficult for them.

ARNOLD.   That's why they've lived in Florence. Porteous has money. They found people there who were willing to accept the situation. (*He moves up a little.*)

ELIZABETH.   This is the first time they've ever come to England.

ARNOLD (*crossing above and to* L. *of the settee*). My father will have to be told, Elizabeth.

ELIZABETH.   Yes.

ANNA (*to* ELIZABETH). Has he ever spoken to you about Lady Kitty ?

ELIZABETH.   Never.

ARNOLD (*above the* L. *end of the settee*). I don't think her name has passed his lips since she ran away from this house thirty years ago.

TEDDIE.   Oh, they lived here ?

ARNOLD.   Naturally. There was a house-party, and one evening neither Porteous nor my mother came down to dinner. The rest of them waited. They couldn't make it out. (*Crossing below the settee to the* R. *chair.*) My father sent up to my mother's room, and a note was found on the pincushion. (*He sits.*)

ELIZABETH (*with a faint smile*). That's what they did in the Dark Ages.

ARNOLD.   I think he took a dislike to this house from that horrible night. He never lived here again, and when I married he handed the place over to me. He just has a cottage now on the estate that he comes to when he feels inclined.

ELIZABETH. It's been very nice for us.

ARNOLD. I owe everything to my father. I don't think he'll ever forgive me for asking these people to come here.

ELIZABETH. I'm going to take all the blame on myself, Arnold.

ARNOLD (*irritably*). The situation was embarrassing enough anyhow. I don't know how I ought to treat them.

ELIZABETH. Don't you think that'll settle itself when you see them ?

ARNOLD. After all, they're my guests. I shall try and behave like a gentleman.

ELIZABETH. I wouldn't. We haven't got central heating.

ARNOLD (*taking no notice*). Will she expect me to kiss her ?

ELIZABETH (*with a smile*). Surely.

ARNOLD (*rising and moving up stage*). It always makes me uncomfortable when people are effusive.

ANNA. But I can't understand why you never saw her before.

ARNOLD. I believe she tried to see me when I was little, but my father thought it better she shouldn't.

ANNA. Yes, but when you were grown up ?

ARNOLD (*moving down to below and* R. *of the chair* R.). She was always in Italy. I never went to Italy.

ELIZABETH. It seems to me so pathetic that if you saw one another in the street you wouldn't recognise each other.

ARNOLD. Is it my fault ?

ELIZABETH (*rising, and moving to* L. *of the* R. *chair*). You've promised to be very gentle with her and very kind.

ARNOLD (*moving up above the* R. *chair*). The mistake was asking Porteous to come too. It looks as though we condoned the whole thing. And how am I to treat him ? Am I to shake him by the hand and slap him on the back ? He absolutely ruined my father's life.

ELIZABETH (*smiling and sitting on the* R. *chair*). How much would you give for a nice motor accident that prevented them from coming ?

ARNOLD (*crossing below the settee to* L.). I let you persuade me against my better judgment, and I've regretted it ever since.

ELIZABETH (*good-humouredly*). I think it's very lucky that Anna and Teddie are here. I don't foresee a very successful party.

ARNOLD (L. *of the settee*). I'm going to do my best. I gave you my promise and I shall keep it. But I can't answer for my father.

(MR. CHAMPION-CHENEY *shows himself at one of the french windows.*)

ANNA (*who has been looking towards the french windows*). Here is your father.

(ELIZABETH *rises and goes up* R.C.)

C.-C. May I come in through the window, or shall I have
myself announced by a supercilious flunkey?

(ARNOLD *moves up* L.C. *a pace or two.* TEDDIE *rises.*)

ELIZABETH.   Come in. We've been expecting you.

C.-.C (*moving down to* ELIZABETH). Impatiently, I hope, my dear
child.

(MR. CHAMPION-CHENEY *is a tall man in the early sixties, spare,
with a fine head of grey hair and an intelligent, somewhat ascetic
face. He is very carefully dressed. He is a man who makes the
most of himself and bears his years jauntily. He kisses* ELIZABETH,
then turns and holds out his hand to ARNOLD.)

How are you, Arnold?   (*They shake hands.*)

(ARNOLD *takes his hat and stick to the table up* L.)

ELIZABETH.   You said you'd be in Paris for another month.

C.-C. (*to* ELIZABETH).   I always reserve to myself the privilege
of changing my mind. It's the only one elderly gentlemen share
with pretty women. (*He takes* ELIZABETH *down to* R. *of the settee.*)

ELIZABETH.   You know Anna.

(ANNA *rises.*)

C.-C. (*below the* R. *end of the settee; shaking hands with her*).
Of course I do. How very nice to see you here ! Are you staying
long ?

ANNA.   As long as I'm welcome. (*She sits at the* R. *end of the
settee.*)

ELIZABETH.   And this is Mr. Luton.

(TEDDIE *moves to* L.C.)

C.-C. (*crossing to* TEDDIE).   How do you do ? Do you play
bridge ?

TEDDIE.   I do.

C.-C.   Capital. Do you declare without top honours ?

TEDDIE.   Never.

C.-C.   Of such is the kingdom of heaven. I see that you are
a good young man.

TEDDIE.   But, like the good in general, I am poor. (*He turns and
sits* L.)

C.-C. (*sitting* L. *of* ANNA).   Never mind ; if your principles are
right, you can play ten shillings a hundred without danger. I never
play for less, and I never play for more.

ARNOLD (*at the* L. *end of the settee*).   And you — are you going
to stay long, father ?

C.-C.   To luncheon, if you'll have me.

(ARNOLD *gives* ELIZABETH *a harassed look.*)

ELIZABETH (R. *of the settee*).   That'll be jolly.

ARNOLD. I didn't mean that. Of course you're going to stay for luncheon. I meant, how long are you going to stay down here ?

C.-C. A week.

(*There is a moment's pause. Everyone but* CHAMPION-CHENEY *is embarrassed.* ARNOLD *crosses above the settee to* R.)

TEDDIE. Well, I think I'll go and tidy up and put the rackets away. (*He rises, moves to the settee table, picks up the rackets.*)

ELIZABETH. Yes. I want my father-in-law to tell me what they are wearing in Paris this week.

(TEDDIE *crosses and exits* L.)

ARNOLD (R. *of the settee*). It's nearly one o'clock, Elizabeth.

ELIZABETH. I didn't know it was so late.

ANNA (*rising and turning to* ARNOLD). I wonder if I can persuade you to take a turn in the garden before luncheon.

ARNOLD (*jumping at the idea*). I'd love it.

(ANNA *goes up to the windows,* ARNOLD *is following her, but he stops irresolutely, and then moves down to the chair* R.)

I want you to look at this chair I've just got. I think it's rather good.

C.-C. Charming. (*He rises and crosses to the chair* R.)

ARNOLD. About 1750, I should say. Good design, isn't it ? It hasn't been restored or anything.

C.-C. Very pretty. (*He turns away* L.)

ARNOLD. I think it was a good buy, don't you ?

C.-C. (*sitting on the* L. *arm of the settee*). Oh, my dear boy, you know I'm entirely ignorant about these things.

ARNOLD. It's exactly my period . . . (*He pauses. Then:*) I shall see you at luncheon, then.

(*He follows* ANNA, *who has waited, into the garden.*)

C.-C. (*standing and breaking a little* L.). Who is that young man ?

ELIZABETH. Mr. Luton. He's the manager of a rubber estate in the F.M.S.

C.-C. (*turning*). And what are the F.M.S. when they're at home ?

ELIZABETH. The Federated Malay States. (*Sitting in the chair* R. *of the settee.*) He's just going back there.

C.-C. (*moving to* C., *in front of the settee*). And why have we been left alone in this very marked manner ?

ELIZABETH. Have we ? I didn't notice it.

C.-C. I suppose it's difficult for the young to realise that one may be old without being a fool.

ELIZABETH. I never thought you that. Everyone knows you're very intelligent.

C.-C. They certainly ought to by now. I've told them often enough. Are you a little nervous ?

ELIZABETH. Let me feel my pulse. (*She puts her finger on her wrist.*) It's perfectly regular.

C.-C. When I suggested staying to luncheon Arnold looked exactly like a dose of castor oil.

ELIZABETH. I wish you'd sit down.

C.-C. Will it make it easier for you ? (*He sits at the* L. *end of the settee*.) You have evidently something very disagreeable to say to me.

ELIZABETH (*rising and moving below the settee*). You won't be cross with me ?

C.-C. How old are you ?

ELIZABETH. Twenty-five.

C.-C. I'm never cross with a woman under thirty.

ELIZABETH. Oh, then I've got ten years. (*She sits* R. *of* CHAMPION-CHENEY.)

C.-C. Mathematics ?

ELIZABETH. No. Paint.

C.-C. Well ? I'm listening.

(*A slight pause.*)

ELIZABETH. Lady Catherine's coming here.

C.-C. Who's Lady Catherine ?

ELIZABETH. Your — Arnold's mother.

C.-C. Is she ?

(*He withdraws himself a little, and* ELIZABETH *gets up.*)

ELIZABETH. You mustn't blame Arnold. It's my fault. I insisted. He was against it. I nagged him till he gave way. And then I wrote and asked her to come.

C.-C. I didn't know you knew her.

ELIZABETH. I don't. But I heard she was in London. She's staying at Claridge's. It seemed so heartless not to take the smallest notice of her.

C.-C. When is she coming ?

ELIZABETH. We're expecting her in time for luncheon.

C.-C. As soon as that ? (*He pats* ELIZABETH's *hand.*) I understand the embarrassment.

ELIZABETH. You see, we never expected you to be here. You said you'd be in Paris for another month.

C.-C. My dear child, this is your house. There's no reason why you shouldn't ask whom you please to stay with you.

ELIZABETH. After all, whatever her faults, she's Arnold's mother. It seemed so unnatural that they should never see one another. My heart ached for that poor lonely woman.

C.-C. I never heard that she was lonely, and she certainly isn't poor.

ELIZABETH. And there's something else. I couldn't ask her by herself. It would have been so — so insulting. I asked Lord Porteous, too.

C.-C. I see.

ELIZABETH. I daresay you'd rather not meet them.

C.-C. I daresay they'd rather not meet me. I shall get a capital luncheon at the cottage. I've noticed you always get the best food if you come in unexpectedly and have the same as they're having in the servants' hall. (*He rises.* ELIZABETH *touches his arm.*)

ELIZABETH. No one's ever talked to me about Lady Kitty. It's always been a subject that everyone has avoided. I've never even seen a photograph of her.

C.-C. The house was full of them when she left. I think I told the butler to throw them in the dust-bin. She was very much photographed.

ELIZABETH. Won't you tell me what she was like ?

C.-C. (*sitting again*). She was very like you Elizabeth, only she had brown hair instead of black.

ELIZABETH. Poor dear ! it must be quite white now.

C.-C. I daresay. She was a pretty little thing.

ELIZABETH. But she was one of the great beauties of her day. They say she was lovely.

C.-C. She had the most adorable little nose, like yours . . .

ELIZABETH. D'you like my nose ?

C.-C. And she was very dainty, with a beautiful little figure ; very light on her feet. She was like a *marquise* in an old French comedy. Yes, she was lovely.

ELIZABETH. And I'm sure she's lovely still.

C.-C. She's no chicken, you know.

ELIZABETH. You can't expect me to look at it as you and Arnold do. When you've loved as she's loved you may grow old, but you grow old beautifully.

C.-C. You're very romantic.

ELIZABETH. If everyone hadn't made such a mystery of it I daresay I shouldn't feel as I do. I know she did a great wrong to you and a great wrong to Arnold. I'm willing to acknowledge that.

C.-C. I'm sure it's very kind of you.

ELIZABETH. But she loved and she dared. Romance is such an elusive thing. You read of it in books, but it's seldom you see it face to face. I can't help it if it thrills me.

C.-C. I am painfully aware that the husband in these cases is not a romantic object.

ELIZABETH. She had the world at her feet. You were rich. She was a figure in society. And she gave up everything for love.

C.-C. (*dryly*). I'm beginning to suspect it wasn't only for her sake and for Arnold's that you asked her to come here.

ELIZABETH. I seem to know her already. I think her face is a little sad, for a love like that doesn't leave you gay, it leaves you grave, but I think her pale face is unlined. It's like a child's.

C.-C. My dear, how you let your imagination run away with you !

ELIZABETH. I imagine her slight and frail.

C.-C. Frail, certainly.

ELIZABETH. With beautiful thin hands and white hair. I've

pictured her so often in that Renaissance Palace that they live in,
with old Masters on the walls and lovely carved things all round,
sitting in a black silk dress with old lace round her neck and old-
fashioned diamonds. You see, I never knew my mother ; she died
when I was a baby. You can't confide in aunts with huge families
of their own. I want Arnold's mother to be a mother to me. I've
got so much to say to her.

C.-C. Are you happy with Arnold ?

ELIZABETH. Why shouldn't I be ?

C.-C. Why haven't you got any babies ?

ELIZABETH. Give us a little time. We've only been married
three years.

C.-C. (*rising and moving up* L.C.). I wonder what Hughie is
like now !

ELIZABETH. Lord Porteous ?

C.-C. He wore his clothes better than any man in London.
You know he'd have been Prime Minister if he'd remained in
politics.

ELIZABETH. What was he like then ?

C.-C. He was a nice-looking fellow. Fine horseman. I suppose
there was something very fascinating about him. Yellow hair and
blue eyes, you know. He had a very good figure. I liked him.
I was his parliamentary secretary. (*Returning to* L. *of the settee.*)
He was Arnold's godfather.

ELIZABETH. I know.

C.-C. I wonder if he ever regrets !

ELIZABETH. I wouldn't.

(*A slight pause.*)

C.-C. (*moving up* L.). Well, I must be strolling back to my cottage.
(*He takes up his hat and stick.*)

ELIZABETH (*rising*). You're not angry with me ? (*She moves
upstage and meets him at* C.)

C.-C. Not a bit.

(ELIZABETH *puts up her face for him to kiss. He kisses her on both
cheeks and then goes into the garden. A pause. A moment
later* TEDDIE *enters* L.)

TEDDIE. I saw the old blighter go.

ELIZABETH. Come in.

TEDDIE. Everything all right ? (*He moves to* L.C.)

ELIZABETH (*moving down* R.). Oh, quite, as far as he's concerned.
He's going to keep out of the way.

TEDDIE (L. *of the settee*). Was it beastly ?

ELIZABETH. No, he made it very easy for me. He's a nice old
thing.

TEDDIE. You were rather scared.

ELIZABETH (*sitting in the chair* R.). A little. I am still. I don't
know why.

TEDDIE. I guessed you were. (*Moving towards her, below the settee.*) I thought I'd come and give you a little moral support. (*He moves up* R.C.) It's ripping here, isn't it ?

ELIZABETH. It is rather nice.

TEDDIE. It'll be jolly to think of it when I'm back in the F.M.S.

ELIZABETH. Aren't you homesick sometimes ?

TEDDIE (*turning to* ELIZABETH). Oh, everyone is now and then, you know.

ELIZABETH. You could have got a job in England if you'd wanted to, couldn't you ?

TEDDIE. · Oh, but I love it out there. England's ripping to come back to, but I couldn't live here now. It's like a woman you're desperately in love with as long as you don't see her, but when you're with her she maddens you so that you can't bear her.

ELIZABETH (*smiling*). What's wrong with England ?

TEDDIE. I don't think anything's wrong with England. I expect something's wrong with me. I've been away too long. (*He moves down* L. *towards the settee.*) England seems to me full of people doing things they don't want to because other people expect it of them.

ELIZABETH. Isn't that what you call a high degree of civilisation ?

TEDDIE. People seem to me so insincere. (*Sitting at the* L. *end of the settee.*) When you go to parties in London they're all babbling about art, and you feel that in their hearts they don't care twopence about it. They read the books that everybody is talking about because they don't want to be out of it. In the F.M.S. we don't get very many books, and we read those we have over and over again. They mean so much to us. (*He pauses.*) I don't think the people over there are half so clever as the people at home, but one gets to know them better. You see, there are so few of us that we have to make the best of one another.

ELIZABETH. I imagine that frills are not much worn in the F.M.S. It must be a comfort.

TEDDIE. It's not much good being pretentious where everyone knows exactly who you are and what your income is.

ELIZABETH. I don't think you want too much sincerity in society. It would be like an iron girder in a house of cards.

TEDDIE. And then, you know, the place is ripping. You get used to a blue sky and you miss it in England.

ELIZABETH. What do you do with yourself all the time ?

TEDDIE. Oh, one works like blazes. You have to be a pretty hefty fellow to be a planter. And then there's ripping bathing. You know, it's lovely, with palm trees all along the beach. And there's shooting. And now and then we have a little dance to a gramophone.

ELIZABETH (*pretending to tease him*). I think you've got a young woman out there, Teddie.

TEDDIE (*vehemently*). Oh, no !

(ELIZABETH *is a little taken aback by the earnestness of his disclaimer. There is a moment's silence, then she recovers herself.*)

ELIZABETH. But you'll have to marry and settle down one of these days, you know.

TEDDIE. I want to, but it's not a thing you can do lightly.

ELIZABETH. I don't know why there more than elsewhere.

TEDDIE. In England if people don't get on they go their own ways and jog along after a fashion. In a place like that you're thrown a great deal on your own resources.

ELIZABETH. Of course.

TEDDIE. Lots of girls come out because they think they're going to have a good time. But if they're empty-headed, then they're just faced with their own emptiness and they're done. (*He rises and moves down* L., *hands in pockets*.) If their husbands can afford it they go home and settle down as grass-widows.

ELIZABETH. I've met them. They seem to find it a very pleasant occupation.

TEDDIE (*moving down below the chair* L.). It's rotten for their husbands, though.

ELIZABETH. And if the husbands can't afford it ?

TEDDIE (*with a gesture — hands out*). Oh, then they tipple.

ELIZABETH. It's not a very alluring prospect.

TEDDIE. But if the woman's the right sort she wouldn't exchange it for any life in the world. When all's said and done it's we who've made the Empire.

ELIZABETH. What sort is the right sort ?

TEDDIE. A woman of courage and endurance and sincerity. (*Taking a step towards* ELIZABETH.) Of course, it's hopeless unless she's in love with her husband.

(*He is looking at her earnestly and she, raising her eyes, gives him a long look. There is silence between them. Then* TEDDIE *sits* C. *of the settee.*)

My house stands on the side of a hill, and the coconut trees wind down to the shore. Azaleas grow in my garden, and camellias, and all sorts of ripping flowers. And in front of me is the winding coast line, and then the blue sea.

(*A pause.*)

Do you know that I'm awfully in love with you ?

ELIZABETH (*gravely*). I wasn't quite sure. I wondered.

TEDDIE. And you ?

(*She nods slowly.*)

I've never kissed you.

ELIZABETH. I don't want you to.

(*They look at one another steadily. They are both grave.* ARNOLD *enters hurriedly at the french windows, and crosses down to* R. *of the settee.*)

ARNOLD. They're coming, Elizabeth.

ELIZABETH (*as though returning from a distant world*). Who ?
ARNOLD (*impatiently*). My dear ! My mother, of course. The
car is just coming up the drive.
TEDDIE (*rising*). Would you like me to clear out ?
ARNOLD. No, No ! For goodness' sake stay.

(TEDDIE *sits again.*)

ELIZABETH (*rising and crossing* L.). We'd better go and meet
them, Arnold.
ARNOLD. No, no ; I think they'd much better be shown in.
(*Moving down* R.) I feel simply sick with nervousness.

(ANNA *comes in from the garden.*)

ANNA. Your guests have arrived. (*She moves into the room.*)
ELIZABETH (*moving up* L.C.). Yes, I know.
ARNOLD (*moving a little down* R.). I've given orders that luncheon
should be served at once.
ELIZABETH. Why ? It's not half-past one already, is it ?
ARNOLD. I thought it would help. When you don't know
exactly what to say you can always eat.

(*The* BUTLER *enters* L. *and announces:*)

BUTLER. Lady Catherine Champion-Cheney ! Lord Porteous !

(TEDDIE *rises, and moves up* R. *of the settee.*)

(LADY KITTY *comes in followed by* PORTEOUS, *and the* BUTLER *goes
out.* LADY KITTY *is a gay little lady, with dyed red hair and
painted cheeks. She is somewhat outrageously dressed. She never
forgets that she has been a pretty woman and still behaves as if
she were twenty-five.* LORD PORTEOUS *is a very bald elderly
gentleman in loose, rather eccentric clothes. He is snappy and gruff.
This is not at all the couple that* ELIZABETH *expected, and for a
moment she stares at them with round, startled eyes.* LADY KITTY
goes to her with outstretched hands.)

LADY KITTY. Elizabeth ! Elizabeth ! (*She kisses her effusively.*)
What an adorable creature ! (*Turning to* PORTEOUS.) Hughie,
isn't she adorable ?
PORTEOUS (*with a grunt*). Ugh ! (*He moves in, to* L.C.)

(ELIZABETH, *smiling now, moves to him and gives him her hand.*)

ELIZABETH. How d'you do ?
PORTEOUS. Damnable road you've got down here. How d'you
do, my dear ? Why d'you have such damnable roads in England ?
(*He moves down* L. *and sits.*)

(LADY KITTY'S *eyes fall on* TEDDIE.)

LADY KITTY. My boy, my boy ! (*She puts her handbag on the
settee table and goes to him, arms outstretched.*) I should have
known you anywhere !

ELIZABETH (*hastily; moving to* L. *of* LADY KITTY). That's Arnold.

LADY KITTY (*without a moment's hesitation*). The image of his father ! (*Crossing* TEDDIE *to* ARNOLD.) I should have known him anywhere ! (*She throws her arms round his neck*.) My boy, my boy !

PORTEOUS (*with a grunt*). Ugh !

LADY KITTY. Tell me, would you have known me again ? Have I changed ?

ARNOLD. I was only five, you know, when — when you . . .

LADY KITTY (*emotionally*). I remember as if it was yesterday. I went up into your room. (*With a sudden change of manner*.) By the way, I always thought that nurse drank. Did you ever find out if she really did ?

PORTEOUS. How the devil can you expect him to know that, Kitty ?

LADY KITTY. You've never had a child, Hughie ; how can you tell what they know and what they don't ?

(*She takes* ARNOLD'*s arm. They move down* C.)

(TEDDIE *moves down* R.)

ELIZABETH (*coming to the rescue*). This is Arnold, Lord Porteous.

(ARNOLD *crosses to* PORTEOUS, *who rises*.)

PORTEOUS (*shaking hands with him*). How d'you do ? I knew your father.

ARNOLD. Yes.

PORTEOUS. Alive still ?

ARNOLD. Yes.

PORTEOUS. He must be getting on. Is he well ?

ARNOLD. Very.

(ELIZABETH *goes to* ANNA. *They move down* R. *of the settee*.)

PORTEOUS. Ugh ! Takes care of himself, I suppose. I'm not at all well. This damned climate doesn't agree with me.

ELIZABETH (*to* LADY KITTY). This is Mrs. Shenstone.

(ANNA *shakes hands with* LADY KITTY *and crosses to* PORTEOUS.)

And this is Mr. Luton.

(TEDDIE *shakes hands with* LADY KITTY. ANNA *has shaken hands with* PORTEOUS *and now sits at the* L. *end of the settee*.)

I hope you don't mind a very small party.

(LADY KITTY *sits at* C. *of the settee*. TEDDIE *sits* R.)

LADY KITTY (*as she sits*). Oh, no, I shall enjoy it. I used to give enormous parties here. Political, you know. How nice you've made this room !

ELIZABETH (*sitting* R. *of* LADY KITTY). Oh, that's Arnold.

(ARNOLD, *who has moved over to* R., *above the settee, moves* TEDDIE *out of the chair* R. TEDDIE *moves up stage.*)

ARNOLD (*nervously*). D'you like this chair ? I've just bought it. It's exactly my period.

PORTEOUS (*bluntly*). It's a fake.

(TEDDIE *moves above the settee to* L. *of it.*)

ARNOLD (*indignantly*). I don't think it is for a minute.

PORTEOUS. The legs are not right.

ARNOLD. I don't know how you can say that. (*Bending over the chair.*) If there is anything right about it, it's the legs.

LADY KITTY. I'm sure they're right.

PORTEOUS. You know nothing whatever about it, Kitty.

LADY KITTY. That's what you think. *I* think it's a beautiful chair. Hepplewhite ?

ARNOLD (*with a little bow*). No, Sheraton.

LADY KITTY. Oh, I know. " The School for Scandal."

PORTEOUS (*turning to the chair* L.). Sheraton, my dear. Sheraton. (*He sits.*)

LADY KITTY. Yes, that's what I say. I acted the screen scene at some amateur theatricals in Florence, and Ermeto Novelli, the great Italian tragedian, told me he'd never seen a Lady Teazle like me.

PORTEOUS. Ugh !

LADY KITTY (*to* ELIZABETH). Do you act ?

ELIZABETH. Oh, I couldn't. I should be too nervous.

LADY KITTY. I'm never nervous. I'm a born actress.

(PORTEOUS *blows his nose.*)

Of course, if I had my time over again I'd go on the stage. You know, it's extraordinary how they keep young. Acresses, I mean. I think it's because they're always playing different parts. Hughie, do you think Arnold takes after me or after his father ? Of course I think he's the very image of me.

(ARNOLD *sits in the chair* R. *of the settee.*)

Arnold, I think I ought to tell you that I was received into the Catholic Church last winter. I'd been thinking about it for years, and last time we were at Monte Carlo I met such a nice monsignore. I told him what my difficulties were and he was too wonderful. I knew Hughie wouldn't approve, so I kept it a secret. (*To* ELIZABETH.) Are you interested in religion ? I think it's too wonderful. We must have a long talk about it one of these days. (*Pointing to her frock.*) Callot ?

ELIZABETH. No, Worth.

LADY KITTY. I knew it was either Worth or Callot. Of course, it's line that's the important thing. I go to Worth myself, and I always say to him, " Line, my dear Worth, line." What *is* the matter, Hughie ?

PORTEOUS. These new teeth of mine are so damned uncomfortable.

LADY KITTY. Men are extraordinary. They can't stand the smallest discomfort. Why, a woman's life is uncomfortable from the moment she gets up in the morning till the moment she goes to bed at night. And d'you think it's comfortable to sleep with a mask on your face ?

PORTEOUS. They don't seem to hold up properly.

LADY KITTY. Well, that's not the fault of your teeth. That's the fault of your gums.

PORTEOUS. Damned rotten dentist. That's what's the matter.

LADY KITTY. I thought he was a very nice dentist. He told me *my* teeth would last till I was fifty. He has a Chinese room. It's so interesting ; while he scrapes your teeth he tells you all about the dear Empress Dowager. Are you interested in China ? I think it's too wonderful. You know they've cut off their pigtails. I think it's such a pity. They were so picturesque.

(*The* BUTLER *enters* R.)

BUTLER. Luncheon is served, sir.

(ARNOLD *rises. The* BUTLER *exits.* ANNA *rises and moves up* R.)

ELIZABETH (*moving to above the* R. *end of the settee*). Would you like to see your rooms ?

PORTEOUS (*rising*). We can see our rooms after luncheon.

LADY KITTY (*rising*). I must powder my nose, Hughie.

PORTEOUS. Powder it down here.

LADY KITTY. I never saw any one so inconsiderate.

PORTEOUS. You'll keep us all waiting half an hour. I know you.

LADY KITTY (*fumbling in her bag*). Oh, well, peace at any price, as Lord Beaconsfield said. (*She sits again.*)

PORTEOUS (*moving a little up* L.C.). He said a lot of damned silly things, Kitty, but he never said that.

(*A pause.* LADY KITTY's *face changes. Perplexity is followed by dismay, and dismay by consternation.*)

LADY KITTY. Oh !

ELIZABETH (*coming to* R. *of* LADY KITTY). What is the matter ?

LADY KITTY (*with anguish*). My lip-stick !

ELIZABETH. Can't you find it ?

(PORTEOUS *comes down to* L. *of the settee.*)

LADY KITTY. I had it in the car. Hughie, you remember that I had it in the car.

PORTEOUS. I don't remember anything about it.

LADY KITTY. Don't be so stupid, Hughie. Why, when we came through the gates I said : " My home, my home ! " and I took it out and put some on my lips.

(PORTEOUS *moves up and above the settee to up* R.C.)

ELIZABETH.   Perhaps you dropped it in the car.

LADY KITTY.   For heaven's sake send someone to look for it.

ARNOLD (*above the chair* R.).   I'll ring.   (*He crosses* R., *and rings the bell.*)

LADY KITTY.   I'm absolutely lost without my lipstick.   Lend me yours, darling, will you ?

(ANNA *moves to the desk up* R.)

ELIZABETH.   I'm awfully sorry.   I'm afraid I haven't got one.

(TEDDIE *moves a little* R.)

LADY KITTY.   Do you mean to say you don't use a lipstick ?

ELIZABETH.   Never.

PORTEOUS (*moving down to the chair* R.).   Look at her lips.   What d'you suppose she wants muck like that for ?   (*He sits.*)

LADY KITTY.   Oh, my dear, what a mistake you make !   You *must* use a lipstick.   It's so good for the lips.   Men like it, you know. I couldn't *live* without a lipstick.

(CHAMPION-CHENEY *appears at the window holding in his upstretched hand a little gold case.*)

C.-C. (*as he moves down,* L. *of the settee*).   Has any one here lost a diminutive utensil containing, unless I am mistaken, a favourite preparation for the toilet ?

(ARNOLD *and* ELIZABETH *are thunderstruck at his appearance and even* TEDDIE *and* ANNA *are taken aback.   But* LADY KITTY *is overjoyed.*)

LADY KITTY.   My lipstick !   (*She moves to* CHAMPION-CHENEY *and takes the lipstick.*)

(ARNOLD *crosses, above the settee, to* L.C.)

C.-C.   I found it in the drive and I ventured to bring it in.

LADY KITTY.   It's Saint Antony.   I said a little prayer to him when I was hunting in my bag.

PORTEOUS.   Saint Antony be blowed !   It's Clive, by God !

(*A slight pause.*)

LADY KITTY (*startled, her attention suddenly turning from the lipstick*).   Clive !

C.-C.   You didn't recognise me.   It's many years since we met.

(ARNOLD *moves up* C., *to the windows.*)

LADY KITTY (*shaking hands*).   My poor Clive, your hair has gone quite white !

C.-C.   I hope you had a pleasant journey down from London.

LADY KITTY (*offering him her cheek*).   You may kiss me, Clive.

C.-C. (*to* PORTEOUS). You don't mind, Hughie ? (*He kisses* LADY KITTY, *who then sits.*)

PORTEOUS (*with a grunt*). Ugh !

C.-C. (*going to* PORTEOUS *cordially*). And how are you, my dear Hughie ?

PORTEOUS (*rising*). Damned rheumatic if you want to know. (*Moving down to below the chair* R.) Filthy climate you have in this country.

C.-C. Aren't you going to shake hands with me, Hughie ?

PORTEOUS. I have no objection to shaking hands with you. (*They shake hands.*)

C.-C. You've aged, my poor Hughie.

PORTEOUS (*working a little up stage*). Someone was asking me how old you were the other day.

C.-C. Were they surprised when you told them ?

PORTEOUS. Surprised ! (*Moving up* R.C.) They wondered you weren't dead.

(*The* FOOTMAN *enters* L.)

FOOTMAN. Did you ring, sir ?

ARNOLD (*moving a little down* L.). No. Oh, yes, I did. It doesn't matter now.

C.-C. (*as the* FOOTMAN *is going*). One moment. My dear Elizabeth, I've come to throw myself on your mercy. My servants are busy with their own affairs. There's not a thing for me to eat in my cottage.

(ARNOLD *moves to* L. *of the settee.*)

ELIZABETH. Oh, but we shall be delighted if you'll lunch with us.

C.-C. It either means that or my immediate death from starvation. You don't mind, Arnold ?

ARNOLD (*moving down a pace*). My dear father . . .

(PORTEOUS *shuffles down a little and looks at* CHAMPION-CHENEY.)

ELIZABETH (*to the* FOOTMAN). Mr. Cheney will lunch here.

FOOTMAN. Very good, ma'am.

(*He crosses* R., *and exits.*)

C.-C. (*crossing to* LADY KITTY). And what do you think of Arnold ? (*He sits on her* R.)

LADY KITTY. I adore him.

C.-C. He's grown, hasn't he ? But then you'd expect him to do that in thirty years.

ARNOLD. For God's sake let's go in to lunch, Elizabeth !

(*As the* CURTAIN *falls*, LADY KITTY *rises and* ARNOLD *takes her up.* ANNA *and* TEDDIE *begin to move* R., *and* ELIZABETH *goes up with* CHAMPION-CHENEY, *who has risen, and* PORTEOUS.)

CURTAIN.

ACT II

The Scene is the same as Act I.

It is afternoon. When the curtain rises, PORTEOUS *and* LADY KITTY, ANNA *and* TEDDIE, *are playing bridge at a table set* L. *of the settee.* PORTEOUS *and* LADY KITTY *are partners.* CHAMPION-CHENEY *stands above the table, watching the game.* ELIZABETH *is sitting* C. *of the settee, with some needlework.*

C.-C. (*moving down to below the settee*). When will Arnold be back, Elizabeth ?

ELIZABETH. Soon, I think.

C.-C. Is he addressing a meeting ?

ELIZABETH. No, it's only a conference with his agent and one or two constituents.

PORTEOUS (*irritably*). How any one can be expected to play bridge when people are shouting at the top of their voices all round them, I for one cannot understand.

ELIZABETH (*smiling*). I'm so sorry.

ANNA. I can see your hand, Lord Porteous.

PORTEOUS. It may help you.

LADY KITTY. I've told you over and over again to hold your cards up. It ruins one's game when one can't help seeing one's opponent's hand.

PORTEOUS. One isn't obliged to look.

LADY KITTY. Elizabeth, what was Arnold's majority at the last election ?

ELIZABETH. Seven hundred and something.

C.-C. (*moving a little down stage*). He'll have to fight for it if he wants to keep his seat next time.

PORTEOUS. Are we playing bridge, or talking politics ?

LADY KITTY. I never find that conversation interferes with my game.

PORTEOUS. You certainly play no worse when you talk than when you hold your tongue.

LADY KITTY. I think that's a very offensive thing to say, Hughie. Just because I don't play the same game as you do you think I can't play. (*She plays an ace.*)

PORTEOUS (*as the game proceeds*). I'm glad you acknowledge it's not the same game as I play. But why in God's name do you call it bridge ?

C.-C. I agree with Kitty. I hate people who play bridge as though they were at a funeral and knew their feet were getting wet.

PORTEOUS. Of course you take Kitty's part.

LADY KITTY. That's the least he can do.

C.-C. I have a naturally cheerful disposition.

24

PORTEOUS. You've never had anything to sour it.

LADY KITTY. I don't know what you mean by that, Hughie. (*She plays a trump.*)

PORTEOUS (*trying to contain himself*). Must you trump my ace?

LADY KITTY (*innocently*). Oh, was that your ace, darling?

PORTEOUS (*furiously*). Yes, it was my ace.

LADY KITTY. Oh, well, it was the only trump I had. I shouldn't have made it anyway.

PORTEOUS. You needn't have told them that. Now she knows exactly what I've got.

LADY KITTY. She knew before.

PORTEOUS. How could she know?

LADY KITTY. She said she'd seen your hand.

ANNA. Oh, I didn't. I said I could see it.

LADY KITTY. Well, I naturally supposed that if she could see it she did.

PORTEOUS. Really, Kitty, you have the most extraordinary ideas.

C.-C. Not at all. If anyone is such a fool as to show me his hand, of course I look at it.

PORTEOUS (*fuming*). If you study the etiquette of bridge, you'll discover that onlookers are expected not to interfere with the game.

C.-C. (*moving up towards the card table*). My dear Hughie, this is a matter of ethics, not of bridge.

ANNA. Anyhow, I get the game. And rubber.

TEDDIE. I claim a revoke.

PORTEOUS. Who revoked?

TEDDIE. You did.

PORTEOUS. Nonsense. I've never revoked in my life.

TEDDIE (*rising*). I'll show you. (*He turns over the tricks to show the faces of the cards.*) You threw away a club on the third heart trick and you had another heart.

(CHAMPION-CHENEY *moves to above* PORTEOUS.)

PORTEOUS. I never had more than two hearts.

TEDDIE. Oh, yes, you had. Look here. That's the card you played on the last trick but one.

LADY KITTY (*delighted to catch him out*). There's no doubt about it, Hughie. You revoked.

PORTEOUS. I tell you I did *not* revoke. I *never* revoke.

C.-C. You did, Hughie. I wondered what on earth you were doing.

PORTEOUS. I don't know how any one can be expected not to revoke when there's this confounded chatter going on all the time.

TEDDIE. Well, that's another hundred to us. (*He moves to the table above the settee for the scoring book.*)

PORTEOUS (*to* CHAMPION-CHENEY). I wish you wouldn't breathe down my neck. I never can play bridge when there's somebody breathing down my neck.

(The party have risen from the bridge table, and they scatter about the room.)

ANNA *(rising)*. Well, I'm going to lie in a hammock and read till it's time to dress. *(She moves below the settee and up* R.C.*)*

TEDDIE *(who has been adding up)*. I'll put it down in the book, shall I ?

PORTEOUS *(who has not moved, setting out the cards for a patience)*. Yes, yes, put it down. I never revoke.

(ANNA goes up C., *and exits to the garden.)*

LADY KITTY. Would you like to come for a little stroll, Hughie ?

PORTEOUS. What for ?

LADY KITTY. Exercise.

PORTEOUS. I hate exercise.

C.-C. *(R. of the card table; looking at the patience)*. The seven goes on the eight.

(PORTEOUS takes no notice.)

LADY KITTY *(looking at the patience)*. The seven goes on the eight, Hughie.

PORTEOUS. I don't choose to put the seven on the eight.

C.-C. That knave goes on the queen.

PORTEOUS. I'm not blind, thank you.

LADY KITTY. The three goes on the four.

C.-C. *(pointing to some of the cards)*. All these go over.

PORTEOUS *(furiously)*. Am I playing this patience, or are you playing it ?

LADY KITTY *(rising)*. But you're missing everything. *(She moves to above and* L. *of* PORTEOUS.*)*

PORTEOUS. That's my business.

C.-C. It's no good losing your temper over it, Hughie.

PORTEOUS. Go away, both of you. You irritate me.

LADY KITTY. We were only trying to help you, Hughie.

PORTEOUS. I don't want to be helped. I want to do it by myself.

LADY KITTY. I think your manners are perfectly deplorable, Hughie.

PORTEOUS. It's simply maddening when you're playing patience and people won't leave you alone.

C.-C. We won't say another word.

(TEDDIE turns up C.*)*

PORTEOUS. That three goes. I believe it's coming out. If I'd been such a fool as to put that seven up I shouldn't have been able to bring these down.

(He puts down several cards while they watch him silently.)

LADY KITTY and C.-C. *(together)*. The four goes on the five.

PORTEOUS (*throwing down the cards violently*). Damn you ! Why don't you leave me alone ? It's intolerable.

C.-C. It was coming out, my dear fellow.

PORTEOUS. I know it was coming out. Confound you !

(ELIZABETH *rises and moves* L.)

LADY KITTY. How petty you are, Hughie !

(CHAMPION-CHENEY *crosses below the settee to* R.)

PORTEOUS. Petty, be damned ! I've told you over and over again that I will not be interfered with when I'm playing patience.

LADY KITTY. Don't talk to me like that, Hughie.

PORTEOUS. I shall talk to you as I please.

LADY KITTY (*beginning to cry*). Oh, you brute ! You brute ! (*She flings out of the room, through the door* L.)

PORTEOUS. Oh, damn ! Now she's going to cry.

(*He rises and shambles out* L.)

(CHAMPION-CHENEY, ELIZABETH *and* TEDDIE *are left alone. There is a moment's pause.* CHAMPION-CHENEY *looks from* TEDDIE *to* ELIZABETH, *with an ironical smile.* ELIZABETH *crosses to the settee and sits* C.)

C.-C. Upon my word, they might be married. (*Sitting* R.) They frip so much.

(TEDDIE *moves to the card table.*)

ELIZABETH (*frigidly*). It's been nice of you to come here so often since they arrived. It's helped to make things easy.

C.-C. Irony ? It's a rhetorical form not much favoured in this blessed plot, this earth, this realm, this England.

ELIZABETH (*taking up her needlework*). What exactly are you getting at ?

C.-C. How slangy the young women of the present day are ! I suppose the fact that Arnold is a purist leads you to the contrary extravagance.

ELIZABETH (*bent over her work*). Anyhow you know what I mean.

C.-C. (*with a smile*). I have a dim, groping suspicion.

ELIZABETH (*looking at him*). You promised to keep away. Why did you come back the moment they arrived ?

C.-C. Curiosity, my dear child. A surely pardonable curiosity.

ELIZABETH. And since then you've been here all the time. You don't generally favour us with so much of your company when you're down at your cottage.

C.-C. I've been excessively amused.

ELIZABETH. It has struck me that whenever they started fripping you took a malicious pleasure in goading them on.

C.-C. I don't think there's much love lost between them now, do you ?

(TEDDIE *is making as though to leave the room.*)

ELIZABETH. Don't go, Teddie.

C.-C. No, please don't.

(TEDDIE *moves to the armchair* L. *of the windows.*)

I'm only staying a minute. We were talking about Lady Kitty just before she arrived. (*To* ELIZABETH.) Do you remember ? The pale, frail lady in black silk and old lace.

ELIZABETH (*with a chuckle, putting down her work*). You are a devil, you know.

C.-C. Ah, well, he's always had the reputation of being a humourist and a gentleman.

ELIZABETH. Did *you* expect her to be like that, poor dear ?

C.-C. My dear child, I hadn't the vaguest idea. You were asking me the other day what she was like when she ran away. I didn't tell you half. She was so gay and so natural. Who would have thought that animation would turn into such frivolity, and that charming impulsiveness lead to such a ridiculous affectation ?

ELIZABETH. It rather sets my nerves on edge to hear the way you talk of her.

C.-C. It's the truth that sets your nerves on edge, not I.

ELIZABETH. You loved her once. Have you no feeling for her at all ?

C.-C. None. Why should I ?

ELIZABETH. She's the mother of your son.

C.-C. My dear child, you have a charming nature, as simple, frank, and artless as hers was. Don't let pure humbug obscure your common sense.

ELIZABETH. We have no right to judge. She's only been here two days. We know nothing about her. (*She bends over her work.*)

C.-C. (*rising and moving to* R. *of the settee*). My dear, her soul is as thickly rouged as her face. She hasn't an emotion that's sincere. She's tinsel. (*Crossing to below the settee.*) You think I'm a cruel, cynical old man. Why, when I think of what she was, if I didn't laugh at what she has become I should cry. (*He turns* L. *of the settee.*)

ELIZABETH (*looking at him*). How do you know she wouldn't be just the same now if she'd remained your wife ? Do you think your influence would have had such a salutary effect on her ?

C.-C. (*good humouredly*). I like you when you're bitter and rather insolent.

ELIZABETH. D'you like me enough to answer my question ?

C.-C. (*sitting on the* L. *end of the settee*). She was only twenty-seven when she went away. She might have become anything. She might have become the woman you expected her to be. There are very few of us who are strong enough to make circumstances serve us. We are the creatures of our environment. She's a silly worthless woman because she's led a silly worthless life.

ELIZABETH (*disturbed*). You're horrible to-day.

C.-C. I don't say it's I who could have prevented her from becoming this ridiculous caricature of a pretty woman grown old. But life could. Here she would have had the friends fit to her station, and a decent activity, and worthy interests. Ask her what her life has been all these years among divorced women and kept women. and the men who consort with them. There is no more lamentable pursuit than a life of pleasure.

ELIZABETH. At all events she loved and she loved greatly. I have only pity and affection for her.

C.-C. And if she loved what d'you think she felt when she saw that she had ruined Hughie ? Look at him. He was tight last night after dinner and tight the night before.

ELIZABETH. I know.

C.-C. And she took it as a matter of course. How long do you suppose he's been getting tight every night ? Do you think he was like that thirty years ago ? Can you imagine that that was a brilliant young man, whom everyone expected to be Prime Minister ? Look at him now. A grumpy sodden old fellow with false teeth.

ELIZABETH. You have false teeth, too.

C.-C. Yes, but damn it all, they fit. (*A slight pause.*) She's ruined him and she knows she's ruined him.

ELIZABETH (*looking at him suspiciously*). Why are you saying all this to me ?

C.-C. Am I hurting your feelings ?

ELIZABETH. I think I've had enough for the present, thank you.

C.-C. (*rising and moving up* L. *of the settee*). I'll go and have a look at the goldfish. I want to see Arnold when he comes in. (*Politely.*) I'm afraid we've been boring Mr. Luton.

TEDDIE (*rising*). Not at all.

(ELIZABETH *rises and moves up* R. *of the settee, carrying her work.*)

C.-C. (*moving to the french windows*). When are you going back to the F.M.S. ?

TEDDIE (*following him*). In about a month.

C.-C. I see.

(CHAMPION-CHENEY *exits.*)

ELIZABETH (*moving up to* TEDDIE). I wonder what he has at the back of his head.

TEDDIE (*moving* R. *to the desk*). Do you think he was talking at you ? (*He stubs his cigarette out at the desk and moves down to the chair* R. *of the settee.*)

ELIZABETH (*moving down*). He's as clever as a bagful of monkeys. (*She puts her needlework on the settee table.*)

(*There is a moment's pause.* TEDDIE *hesitates a little and when he speaks it is in a different tone. He is grave and somewhat nervous.*)

TEDDIE.   It seems very difficult to get a few minutes alone with you. I wonder if you've been making it difficult ?

ELIZABETH (*turning towards* L.C.)   I wanted to think.

TEDDIE.   I've made up my mind to go away tomorrow.

ELIZABETH (*moving down to the* L. *end of the settee*).   Why ?

TEDDIE.   I want you altogether or not at all.

ELIZABETH.   You're so arbitrary.

TEDDIE (*taking a step towards the settee*).   You said you — you cared for me.

ELIZABETH.   I do.

TEDDIE.   Do you mind if we talk it over now ?

ELIZABETH.   No. (*She sits at the* L. *end of the settee*.)

TEDDIE (*frowning*).   It makes me feel rather shy and awkward.

(ELIZABETH *looks at* TEDDIE.)

I've repeated to myself over and over again exactly what I want to say to you, (*turning down to the chair* R.) and now all I'd prepared seems rather footling.

ELIZABETH.   I'm so afraid I'm going to cry.

TEDDIE.   I feel it's all so tremendously serious and I think we ought to keep emotion out of it. You're rather emotional, aren't you ?

ELIZABETH (*half smiling and half in tears*).   So are you for the matter of that.

TEDDIE (*crossing to the settee*).   That's why I wanted to have everything I meant to say to you cut and dried. (*He sits* R. *of* ELIZABETH.)   I think it would be awfully unfair if I made love to you and all that sort of thing, and you were carried away. I wrote it all down and thought I'd send it you as a letter.

ELIZABETH.   Why didn't you ?

TEDDIE.   I got rather scared. A letter seems so — so cold. You see, I love you so awfully.

ELIZABETH.   For goodness' sake don't say that.

TEDDIE.   You musn't cry. (*Rising.*)   Please don't, or I shall go all to pieces.

ELIZABETH (*trying to smile*).   I'm sorry. It doesn't mean anything really. It's only tears running out of my eyes.

TEDDIE.   Our only chance is to be awfully matter-of-fact. (*He stops for a moment.   He finds it quite difficult to control himself.   He clears his throat.   He frowns with annoyance at himself.*)

ELIZABETH.   What's the matter ?

TEDDIE (*turning up* R., *to above the settee*).   I've got a sort of lump in my throat. It is idiotic. I think I'll have a cigarette.

(*A pause.* ELIZABETH *looks at* TEDDIE *in silence.*)

You see, I've never been in love with anyone before, not really. It's knocked me endways. I don't know how I can live without you now . . . (*He takes out a cigarette.*)   Does that old fool know I'm in love with you ?

ELIZABETH. I think so.

TEDDIE. When he was talking about Lady Kitty smashing up Lord Porteous' career I thought there was something at the back of it. (*He puts the cigarette back into the case, turning away from* ELIZABETH.)

ELIZABETH. I think he was trying to persuade me not to smash up yours.

TEDDIE (*moving down* R. *of the settee*). I'm sure that's very considerate of him, but I don't happen to have one to smash. I wish I had. It's the only time in my life I've wished I were a hell of a swell so that I could chuck it all (*he sits* R. *of* ELIZABETH) and show you how much more you are to me than anything else in the world.

ELIZABETH (*affectionately*). You're a dear thing, Teddie.

TEDDIE. You know, I don't really know how to make love, but if I did I couldn't do it now because I just want to be absolutely practical.

ELIZABETH (*chaffing him*). I'm glad you don't know how to make love. It would be almost more than I could bear.

TEDDIE. You see, I'm not at all romantic and that sort of thing. I'm just a common or garden business man. All this is so dreadfully serious and I think we ought to be sensible.

ELIZABETH (*with a break in her voice*). You owl !

TEDDIE. No, Elizabeth, don't say things like that to me. I want you to consider all the *pros* and *cons*, and my heart's thumping against my chest, and you know I love you, I love you, I love you.

ELIZABETH (*in a sigh of passion*). Oh, my precious.

TEDDIE (*turning away; impatiently, but with himself, rather than with Elizabeth*). Don't be idiotic, Elizabeth. I'm not going to tell you that I can't live without you and a lot of muck like that. (*Turning to face her.*) You know that you mean everything in the world to me. (*Almost giving it up as a bad job.*) Oh, my God !

ELIZABETH (*her voice faltering*). D'you think there's anything you can say to me that I don't know already ?

TEDDIE (*desperately*). But I haven't said a single thing I wanted to. I'm a business man and I want to put it all in a business way, if you understand what I mean.

ELIZABETH (*smiling*). I don't believe you're a very good business man.

TEDDIE (*sharply*). You don't know what you're talking about. I'm a first-rate business man, but somehow this is different. (*Hopelessly, as he rises.*) I don't know why it won't go right. (*He turns away* R.)

(*A pause.*)

ELIZABETH (*rising*). What are we going to do about it ?

TEDDIE (*turning back to her*). You see, it's not just because you're awfully pretty that I love you. I'd love you just as much if you were old and ugly. It's you I love, not what you look like. And it's not

only love ; love be blowed ! It's that I *like* you so tremendously.
I think you're such a ripping good sort. I just want to be with you.
I feel so jolly and happy just to think you're there. I'm so awfully
fond of you.

ELIZABETH (*laughing through her tears*). I don't know if this is
your idea of introducing a business proposition.

TEDDIE. Damn you, you won't let me.

ELIZABETH. You said " Damn you."

TEDDIE. I meant it.

ELIZABETH. Your voice sounded as if you meant it, you perfect
duck.

TEDDIE (*crossing below the settee to down* L.). Really, Elizabeth,
you're intolerable.

ELIZABETH (*turning to him*). I'm doing nothing.

TEDDIE (*moving towards her*). Yes, you are, you're putting me
off my blow.

(ELIZABETH *sits on the settee.*)

What I want to say is perfectly simple. I'm a very ordinary
business man.

ELIZABETH. You've said that before.

TEDDIE (*angrily*). Shut up. (*Moving to above the card table.*)
I haven't got a bob besides what I earn. I've got no position. I'm
nothing. You're rich and you're a big pot and you've got everything
that anyone can want. It's awful cheek my saying anything to you
at all. (*Sitting on the chair* R. *of the table.*) But after all there's
only one thing that really matters in the world, and that's love.
I love you. Chuck all this, Elizabeth, and come to me.

ELIZABETH (*turning to look at* TEDDIE). Are you cross with me ?

TEDDIE. Furious.

ELIZABETH. Darling !

TEDDIE (*rising and turning away* L.). If you don't want me tell
me so at once and let me get out quickly.

ELIZABETH (*rising and crossing to* TEDDIE). Teddie, nothing in
the world matters anything to me but you.

(TEDDIE *turns to her.*)

I'll go wherever you take me. I love you.

TEDDIE (*all to pieces*). Oh, my God ! (*He collapses in the chair* L.)

ELIZABETH. Does it mean as much to you as that ? Oh, Teddie !

TEDDIE (*trying to control himself*). Don't be a fool, Elizabeth.

ELIZABETH. It's you're the fool. (*She moves away a little* R.)
You're making me cry.

TEDDIE. You're so damned emotional.

ELIZABETH (*crossing below the settee to* C.). Damned emotional
yourself. I'm sure you're a rotten business man.

TEDDIE (*rising and moving towards her*). I don't care what you
think. You've made me so awfully happy. I say, what a lark life's
going to be !

ELIZABETH. Teddie, you are an angel.

TEDDIE. Let's get out quick. It's no good wasting time. Elizabeth.

ELIZABETH. What ?

TEDDIE. Nothing. I just like to say Elizabeth.

ELIZABETH. You fool !

TEDDIE. I say, can you shoot ?

ELIZABETH. No.

TEDDIE. I'll teach you. (*They both sit on the settee.*) You don't know how ripping it is to start out from your camp at dawn and travel through the jungle. And you're so tired at night and the sky's all starry. Of course, I didn't want to say anything about all that till you'd decided. I'd made up my mind to be absolutely practical.

ELIZABETH (*chaffing him*). The only practical thing you said was that love is the only thing that really matters.

TEDDIE (*happily*). Pull the other leg next time, will you ? I should hate to have one longer than the other.

ELIZABETH (*giving* TEDDIE *both her hands*). Isn't it fun being in love with someone who's in love with you ?

TEDDIE. I say, I think I'd better clear out at once, don't you ? It seems rather rotten to stay on in — in this house.

ELIZABETH. You can't go tonight. There's no train.

TEDDIE. I'll go tomorrow. I'll wait in London till you're ready to join me.

ELIZABETH (*rising*). I'm not going to leave a note on the pincushion like Lady Kitty, you know. (*Moving a little* R.) I'm going to tell Arnold.

TEDDIE. Are you ? Don't you think there'll be an awful bother ?

ELIZABETH (*turning to him*). I must face it. I should hate to be sly and deceitful.

TEDDIE. Well, then, let's face it together.

ELIZABETH (*moving a little towards him*). No, I'll talk to Arnold by myself.

TEDDIE (*rising*). You won't let anyone influence you ?

ELIZABETH. No.

(TEDDIE *holds out his hand and she takes it. They look into one another's eyes with grave, almost solemn affection. There is the sound outside of a car driving up.*)

ELIZABETH (*moving a step down*). There's the car. Arnold's come back. (*She crosses to the door* L.) I must go and bathe my eyes. I don't want them to see I've been crying. (*She opens the door.*)

TEDDIE. All right. (*As she is going.*) Elizabeth.

ELIZABETH (*turning*). What ?

TEDDIE. Bless you.

ELIZABETH (*affectionately*). Idiot !

(*She exits* L.)

C

(TEDDIE *goes up and through the french window into the garden.*)

(*For an instant the room is empty.* ARNOLD *comes in* L. *He crosses* R. *to the desk and takes some papers out of his despatch-case.* LADY KITTY *enters.*)

LADY KITTY. I saw you come in.

(ARNOLD *rises.*)

Oh, my dear, don't get up. There's no reason why you should be so dreadfully polite to me.

ARNOLD. I've just rung for a cup of tea.

LADY KITTY (*moving across to up* C.). Perhaps we shall have the chance of a little talk. We don't seem to have had five minutes by ourselves. I want to make your acquaintance, you know.

(*They both move down* R.C.)

ARNOLD. I should like you to know that it's not by my wish that my father is here.

LADY KITTY. But I'm so interested to see him. (*She brings* ARNOLD *down* R. *of the settee to below it.*)

ARNOLD. I was afraid that you and Lord Porteous must find it embarrassing.

LADY KITTY. Oh, no.

(*She sits. Then* ARNOLD *sits on her* R.)

Hughie was his greatest friend. They were at Eton and Oxford together. I think your father has improved so much since I saw him last. He wasn't good-looking as a young man, but now he's quite handsome.

(*The* BUTLER *and* FOOTMAN *enter* L. *They carry a low table, and a tray on which are tea things for two. They set the table and tea down* C., *below the settee, and then exeunt* L.)

LADY KITTY. Shall I pour it out for you ?

ARNOLD. Thank you very much.

LADY KITTY (*doing so*). Do you take sugar ?

ARNOLD. No. I gave it up during the war.

LADY KITTY. So wise of you. It's so bad for the figure. (*Giving* ARNOLD *a cup.*) Besides being patriotic, of course. Isn't it absurd that I should ask my son if he takes sugar or not ? (*Pouring her own tea.*) Life is really very quaint. Sad, of course, but oh, so quaint ! Often I lie in bed at night and have a good laugh to myself as I think how quaint life is.

ARNOLD. I'm afraid I'm a very serious person. (*He sips his tea.*)

LADY KITTY. How old are you now, Arnold ? (*She drinks her tea.*)

ARNOLD. Thirty-five.

LADY KITTY. Are you really ? Of course, I was a child when I married your father.

ARNOLD.   Really.   He always told me you were twenty-two.
(*He drinks his tea.*)

LADY KITTY.   Oh, what nonsense !   Why, I was married out of
the nursery.   (*Taking the cup from* ARNOLD.)   I put my hair up for
the first time on my wedding-day.

(*A pause.*)

ARNOLD.   Where is Lord Porteous ?

LADY KITTY.   My dear, it sounds too absurd to hear you call
him Lord Porteous.   Why don't you call him — Uncle Hughie ?

ARNOLD.   He doesn't happen to be my uncle.

LADY KITTY.   No, but he's your godfather.   You know, I'm
sure you'll like him when you know him better.   I'm so hoping that
you and Elizabeth will come and stay with us in Florence.   I simply
adore Elizabeth.   She's too beautiful.

ARNOLD.   Her hair is very pretty.

LADY KITTY.   It's not touched up, is it ?

ARNOLD.   Oh, no.

LADY KITTY.   I just wondered.   It's rather a coincidence that
her hair should almost be the same colour as mine.   I suppose it
shows that your father and you are attracted by just the same thing.
So interesting, heredity, isn't it ?

ARNOLD.   Very.

LADY KITTY.   Of course, since I joined the Catholic Church
I don't believe in it any more.   Darwin and all that sort of thing.
Too dreadful.   Wicked, you know.   Besides, it's not very good form,
is it ?

(CHAMPION-CHENEY *enters up* C. *from the garden.*)

C.-C.   Do I intrude ?   (*He crosses down to above the* R. *end of
the settee.*)

LADY KITTY.   Come in, Clive   Arnold and I have been having
such a wonderful heart-to-heart talk.

C.-C.   Very nice.

(ARNOLD *rises and moves to the chair* R.)

ARNOLD.   Father, I stepped in for a moment at the Harveys'
on my way back.   (*Moving above the chair.*)   It's simply criminal
what they're doing with that house.

C.-C.   What are they doing ?

ARNOLD.   It's an almost perfect Georgian house and they've
got a lot of dreadful Victorian furniture.   I gave them my ideas
on the subject, but it's quite hopeless.   They said they were attached
to their furniture.

C.-C.   Arnold should have been an interior decorator.   (*He
sits* R. *of* LADY KITTY.)

LADY KITTY.   He has wonderful taste.   He gets that from me.

ARNOLD.   I suppose I have a certain *flair*.   I have a passion for
decorating houses.

LADY KITTY. You've made this one charming.

C.-C. D'you remember, we just had chintzes and comfortable chairs when we lived here, Kitty.

LADY KITTY. Perfectly hideous, wasn't it ?

C.-C. In those days gentlemen and ladies were not expected to have taste.

ARNOLD (*sitting in the chair down* R. *below the door*). You know, I've been looking at this chair again. Since Lord Porteous said the legs weren't right I've been very uneasy. (*He looks at the legs of the chair* R. *of the settee.*)

LADY KITTY. He only said that because he was in a bad temper.

C.-C. His temper seems to me very short these days, Kitty.

LADY KITTY. Oh, it is.

ARNOLD (*rising and moving up a little*). You feel he knows what he's talking about. I gave seventy-five pounds for that chair. I'm very seldom taken in. I always think if a thing's right you feel it.

C.-C. Well, don't let it disturb your night's rest.

ARNOLD (*moving to* R. *of the settee*). But, my dear father, that's just what it does. I had a most horrible dream about it last night.

(*Enter* PORTEOUS L.)

(*Moving to the chair again*). I'm going to fetch a book I have on Old English furniture. There's an illustration of a chair which is almost identical with this one.

PORTEOUS (*moving to the chair* L. *of the card table*). Quite a family gathering, by George !

C.-C. I was thinking just now we'd make a very pleasing picture of a typical English home.

ARNOLD (*moving to* L.C.). I'll be back in five minutes. There's something I want to show you, Lord Porteous.

(*He exits* L.)

(*Enter the* FOOTMAN L. *He crosses down to take the tea tray away. As he moves up with it,* PORTEOUS *takes the bread and butter away and sits* L. *of the card table.*)

(*The* FOOTMAN *exits* L. *with the tray.*)

C.-C. Would you like to play piquet with me, Hughie ?

PORTEOUS. Not particularly.

C.-C. You were never much of a piquet player, were you ?

PORTEOUS. My dear Clive, you people don't know what piquet is in England.

C.-C. (*half rising*). Let's have a game then. You may make money.

PORTEOUS. I don't want to play with you.

(CHAMPION-CHENEY *sits again.*)

LADY KITTY. I don't know why not, Hughie.

PORTEOUS. Let me tell you that I don't like your manner.

C.-C. I'm sorry for that. I'm afraid I can't offer to change it at my age.

PORTEOUS. I don't know what you want to be hanging around here for.

C.-C. A natural attachment to my home.

PORTEOUS. If you'd had any tact you'd have kept out of the way while we were here.

C.-C. My dear Hughie, I don't understand your attitude at all. If I'm willing to let bygones be bygones why should you object ?

PORTEOUS (*rising*). Damn it all, they're not bygones.

C.-C. After all, I am the injured party.

PORTEOUS (*moving a step down towards the settee*). How the devil are you the injured party ?

C.-C. Well, you did run away with my wife, didn't you ?

LADY KITTY. Now, don't let's go into ancient history. I don't see why we shouldn't all be friends.

PORTEOUS (*turning away*). I beg you not to interfere, Kitty.

LADY KITTY. I'm very fond of Clive.

PORTEOUS (*turning back to her*). You never cared two straws for Clive. You only say that to irritate me. (*He moves to* L. *of the settee.*)

LADY KITTY. Not at all. I don't see why he shouldn't come and stay with us.

C.-C. I'd love to. I think Florence in spring-time is delightful. Have you central heating ?

PORTEOUS. I never *liked* you, I *don't* like you *now*, and I *never shall* like you.

C.-C. How very unfortunate ! Because I liked you, I like you now, and I shall continue to like you.

LADY KITTY. There's something very nice about you, Clive.

PORTEOUS. If you think that, why the devil did you leave him ?

LADY KITTY. Are you going to reproach me because I loved you ? (*Rising and moving away* R. *of the settee.*) How utterly, utterly, utterly detestable you are !

C.-C. Now, now, don't quarrel with one another.

LADY KITTY. It's all his fault. I'm the easiest person in the world to live with. (*She sits in the chair* R. *of the settee.*) But really he'd try the patience of a saint.

C.-C. Come, come, don't get upset, Kitty. When two people live together there must be a certain amount of give and take.

PORTEOUS (*to below the settee*). I don't know what the devil you're talking about. (*He sits* C. *on the settee.*)

C.-C. It hasn't escaped my observation that you are a little inclined to frip. Many couples are. I think it's a pity.

PORTEOUS (*rising and sitting again*). Would you have the very great kindness to mind your own business ?

LADY KITTY. It is his business. He naturally wants me to be happy.

C.-C. I have the very greatest affection for Kitty.

PORTEOUS.   Then why the devil didn't you look after her properly?

C.-C.   My dear Hughie, you were my greatest friend. I trusted you. It may have been rash.

PORTEOUS.   It was inexcusable.

LADY KITTY (*rising*).   I don't know what you mean by that, Hughie.

PORTEOUS.   Don't, don't, don't try and bully me, Kitty.

LADY KITTY (*moving above the settee towards the card table*). Oh, I know what you mean.

PORTEOUS.   Then why the devil did you say you didn't ?

LADY KITTY.   When I think that I sacrificed everything for that man ! And for thirty years I've had to live in a filthy marble palace with no sanitary conveniences. (*She moves up stage.*)

C.-C.   D'you mean to say you haven't got a bathroom ?

LADY KITTY (*moving down a pace*).   I've had to wash in a tub. (*She sits in the L. chair above the card table.*)

C.-C.   My poor Kitty, how you've suffered !

PORTEOUS.   Really, Kitty, I'm sick of hearing of the sacrifices you made. I suppose you think I sacrificed nothing. I should have been Prime Minister by now if it hadn't been for you.

LADY KITTY.   Nonsense !

PORTEOUS.   What do you mean by that ? Everyone said I should be Prime Minister. Shouldn't I have been Prime Minister, Clive ?

C.-C.   It was certainly the general expectation.

PORTEOUS.   I was the most promising young man of my day. I was bound to get a seat in the Cabinet at the next election.

LADY KITTY (*rising and moving to L. of the settee*).   They'd have found you out just as I've found you out. (*Crossing back below the settee to R. of it.*) I'm sick of hearing that I ruined your career. (*Turning to face PORTEOUS.*) You never had a career to ruin. Prime Minister ! You haven't the brain. You haven't the character.

C.-C.   Cheek, push, and a gift of the gab will serve very well instead, you know.

LADY KITTY (*moving to behind CHAMPION-CHENEY*).   Besides, in politics it's not the men that matter. It's the women at the back of them. (*Putting her hands on CHAMPION-CHENEY's shoulders.*) I could have made Clive a Cabinet Minister if I'd wanted to.

PORTEOUS.   Clive ?

LADY KITTY.   With my beauty, my charm, my force of character, my wit, I could have done anything. (*She turns and sits on the chair down R.*)

PORTEOUS.   Clive was nothing but my political secretary. When I was Prime Minister I might have made him Governor of some Colony or other. Western Australia, say. Out of pure kindliness.

LADY KITTY (*with flashing eyes*).   D'you think I would have buried myself in Western Australia ? With my beauty ? My charm ?

PORTEOUS.   Or Barbadoes, perhaps.

LADY KITTY (*furiously; rising*).   Barbadoes ! Barbadoes can go to — (*sitting again*) Barbadoes.

PORTEOUS. That's all you'd have got.

KITTY. Nonsense ! I'd have had India.

PORTEOUS (*rising*). I would never have given you India.

LADY KITTY. You would have given me India.

PORTEOUS. I tell you I wouldn't.

LADY KITTY. The King would have given me India. (*She rises again.*) The nation would have insisted on my having India. I would have been a vice-reine or nothing. (*She crosses up to the desk.*)

PORTEOUS. I tell you that as long as the interests of the British Empire — Damn it all, my teeth are coming out !

(*He hurries out of the room at* L.)

(CHAMPION-CHENEY *rises and moves to below* C. *of the settee.*)

LADY KITTY. It's too much. I can't bear it any more. (*She turns the desk chair and sits.*) I've put up with him for thirty years and now I'm at the end of my tether.

C.-C. (*sitting*). Calm yourself, my dear Kitty.

LADY KITTY. I won't listen to a word. I've quite made up my mind. It's finished, finished, finished. (*With a change of tone.*) I was so touched when I heard that you never lived in this house again after I left it.

C.-C. The cuckoos have always been very plentiful. Their note has a personal application which, I must say, I have found extremely offensive.

LADY KITTY. When I saw that you didn't marry again I couldn't help thinking that you still loved me. (*She rises and moves down* R. *of the settee.*)

C.-C. I am one of the few men I know who is able to profit by experience.

LADY KITTY (*to below the settee*). In the eyes of the Church I am still your wife. (*Sitting* R. *of* CHAMPION-CHENEY.) The Church is so wise. It knows that in the end a woman always comes back to her first love. Clive, I am willing to return to you.

C.-C. My dear Kitty, I couldn't take advantage of your momentary vexation with Hughie to let you take a step which I know you would bitterly regret.

LADY KITTY. You've waited for me a long time. For Arnold's sake.

C.-C. Do you think we really need bother about˙ Arnold ? In the last thirty years he's had time to grow used to the situation.

LADY KITTY (*with a little smile*). I think I've sown my wild oats, Clive.

C.-C. I haven't. I was a good young man, Kitty.

LADY KITTY. I know.

C.-C. And I'm very glad, because it has enabled me to be a wicked old one.

LADY KITTY. I beg your pardon.

(ARNOLD *re-enters with a large book in his hand. He moves to* L. *of the settee.*)

ARNOLD. I say, I've found the book I was hunting for. Oh ! isn't Lord Porteous here ?

LADY KITTY. One moment, Arnold. Your father and I are busy.

Arnold (*turning*). I'm so sorry.

(*He exits* L.)

LADY KITTY. Explain yourself, Clive.

C.-C. When you ran away from me, Kitty, I was sore and angry and miserable. But above all I felt a fool.

LADY KITTY. Men are so vain.

C.-C. But I was a student of history, and presently I reflected that I shared my misfortune with very nearly all the greatest men.

LADY KITTY. I'm a great reader myself. It has always struck me as peculiar.

C.-C. The explanation is very simple. Women dislike intelligence and when they find it in their husbands they revenge themselves on them in the only way they can, by making them — well, what you made me.

LADY KITTY. It's ingenious. It may be true.

C.-C. I felt I had done my duty by society and I determined to devote the rest of my life to my own entertainment. The House of Commons had always bored me excessively and the scandal of our divorce gave me an opportunity to resign my seat. I have been relieved to find that the country got on perfectly well without me.

LADY KITTY. But has love never entered your life ?

C.-C. Tell me frankly, Kitty, don't you think people make a lot of unnecessary fuss about love ?

LADY KITTY. It's the most wonderful thing in the world.

C.-C. (*laughing*). You're incorrigible. Do you really think it was worth sacrificing so much for ?

LADY KITTY. My dear Clive, I don't mind telling you that if I had my time over again I should be unfaithful to you, but I should not leave you.

C.-C. (*settling down in the* L. *corner of the settee*). For some years I was notoriously the prey of a secret sorrow. But I found so many charming creatures who were anxious to console that in the end it grew rather fatiguing. Out of regard to my health I ceased to frequent the drawing-rooms of Mayfair.

LADY KITTY. And since then ?

C.-C. Since then I have allowed myself the luxury of assisting financially a succession of dear little things, in a somewhat humble sphere, between the ages of twenty and twenty-five.

LADY KITTY. I cannot understand the infatuation of men for young girls. I think they're so dull.

C.-C. (*patting her hand*). It's a matter of taste. I love old wine, old friends and old books, but I like young women. On their twenty-fifth birthday I give them a diamond ring and tell them they must no longer waste their youth and beauty on an old fogey like me. We have a most affecting scene, my technique on these occasions is perfect, and then I start all over again.

LADY KITTY. You're a wicked old man, Clive.

C.-C. That's what I told you. But, by George, I'm a happy one.

LADY KITTY (*rising and crossing* L.). There's only one course open to me now.

C.-C. (*rising*). What is that ?

(*A slight pause.* LADY KITTY *turns to him.*)

LADY KITTY (*with a flashing smile*). To go and dress for dinner. (*She turns to the doors* L.)

C.-C. Capital. I will follow your example. (*He moves* R.)

(*As* LADY KITTY *goes* L. ELIZABETH *enters.* LADY KITTY *exits.*)

ELIZABETH (*to* L.C.). Where is Arnold ?

CHAMPION-CHENEY (*turning*). He was here a moment ago. Shall I go and look for him ?

ELIZABETH (*crossing below the settee to the* R. *end of it*). Don't bother. (*She sits.*)

(*Enter* ARNOLD L. *He carries a book.*)

CHAMPION-CHENEY. Oh, here he is.

ARNOLD. Hullo.

CHAMPION-CHENEY. I was just strolling along to my cottage to put on a dinner jacket.

(*He exits to the garden.*)

ARNOLD (*moving to below the settee*). Oh, Elizabeth, I've found an illustration here of a chair which is almost identical with mine. (*Sitting on her* L.) It's dated 1750. Look !

ELIZABETH. That's very interesting.

ARNOLD (*putting down the book, rising and moving* R.). I want to show it to Porteous. (*Adjusting the chair which has been misplaced.*) You know, it does exasperate me the way people will not leave things alone. I no sooner put a thing in its place than somebody moves it.

ELIZABETH. It must be maddening for you.

ARNOLD. It is. You are the worst offender. (*Moving to* R. *of the settee.*) I can't think why you don't take the pride that I do in the house. After all, it's one of the show places in the county. (*He moves to below the chair* R. *of the settee.*)

ELIZABETH. I'm afraid you find me very unsatisfactory.

ARNOLD (*good-humouredly*). I don't know about that. (*Moving a little up stage.*) But my two subjects are politics and decoration. I should be a perfect fool if I didn't *see* that you don't care two straws about either.

ELIZABETH. We haven't very much in common, Arnold, have we?

ARNOLD. I don't think you can blame me for that.

ELIZABETH. I don't. (*Rising.*) I blame you for nothing. I have no fault to find with you.

ARNOLD (*surprised at her significant tone*). Good gracious me ! (*With a step towards her.*) What's the meaning of all this ?

ELIZABETH (*moving away to the chair* L. *of the card table*). Well, I don't think there's any object in beating about the bush. (*Turning to* ARNOLD.) I want you to let me go.

ARNOLD. Go where ?

ELIZABETH. Away. For always.

ARNOLD (*moving below the settee to* C.). My dear child, what *are* you talking about ?

ELIZABETH. I want to be free.

ARNOLD (*amused rather than disconcerted*). Don't be ridiculous, darling. I daresay you're run down and want a change. I'll take you over to Paris for a fortnight if you like. (*He sits at the* R. *end of the settee.*)

ELIZABETH (*moving down towards* ARNOLD). I shouldn't have spoken to you if I hadn't quite made up my mind. We've been married for three years and I don't think it's been a great success. I'm frankly bored by the life you want me to lead.

ARNOLD. Well, if you'll allow me to say so, the fault is yours. We lead a very distinguished, useful life. We know a lot of extremely nice people.

ELIZABETH. I'm quite willing to allow that the fault is mine. But how does that make it any better ? I'm only twenty-five. If I've made a mistake I have time to correct it.

ARNOLD. I can't bring myself to take you very seriously. (*He takes up the book.*)

ELIZABETH. You see, I don't love you.

ARNOLD (*looking through the book*). Well, I'm awfully sorry. But you weren't obliged to marry me. You've made your bed and I'm afraid you must lie on it.

ELIZABETH. That's one of the falsest proverbs in the English language. Why should you lie on the bed you've made if you don't want to ? There's always the floor.

ARNOLD (*closing the book*). For goodness' sake don't be funny, Elizabeth.

ELIZABETH. I've quite made up my mind to leave you, Arnold.

ARNOLD (*putting the book down on the settee*). Come, come, Elizabeth, you must be sensible. You haven't any reason to leave me.

ELIZABETH. Why should you wish to keep a woman tied to you who wants to be free ?

ARNOLD. I happen to be in love with you.

ELIZABETH. You might have said that before.

ARNOLD. I thought you'd take it for granted. You can't expect a man to go on making love to his wife after three years. I'm very busy. I'm awfully keen on politics and I've worked like a dog to

make this house a thing of beauty. After all, a man marries to have
a home, but also because he doesn't want to be bothered with sex
and all that sort of thing. I fell in love with you the first time I saw
you and I've been in love ever since.

ELIZABETH. I'm sorry, but if you're not in love with a man his
love doesn't mean very much to you. (*She moves to a chair* R. *of
the card table, and sits.*)

ARNOLD. It's so ungrateful. I've done everything in the world
for you.

ELIZABETH. You've been very kind to me. (*Turning to him.*)
But you've asked me to lead a life I don't like and that I'm not
suited for.

(ARNOLD *rises.*)

I'm awfully sorry to cause you pain, but now you must let me go·

ARNOLD (*crossing to* L. *of the settee*). Nonsense ! I'm a good
deal older than you are and I think I have a little more sense. In
your interests as well as in mine I'm not going to do anything of
the sort.

ELIZABETH (*with a smile*). How can you prevent me ? You can't
keep me under lock and key.

ARNOLD. Please don't talk to me as if I were a foolish child.
You're my wife and you're going to remain my wife.

ELIZABETH. What' sort of a life do you think we should lead ?
Do you think there'd be any more happiness for you than for me ?

ARNOLD. But what is it precisely that you suggest ?

ELIZABETH. Well, I want you to let me divorce you.

ARNOLD (*astounded*). Me ? Thank you very much. Are you
under the impression I'm going to sacrifice my career for a whim
of yours ?

ELIZABETH. How will it do that?

ARNOLD. My majority is shaky enough as it is. Do you think
I'd be able to hold it if I were in a divorce case ? Even if it were
a put-up job, as most divorces are nowadays, it would damn me.

ELIZABETH (*gazing front*). It's rather hard on a woman to be
divorced.

ARNOLD (*with sudden suspicion*). What do you mean by that ?
(*Taking a step towards her.*) Are you in love with someone ?

ELIZABETH. Yes.

ARNOLD. Who ?

ELIZABETH. Teddie Luton.

(ARNOLD *is astonished for a moment, then bursts into a laugh.*)

ARNOLD. My poor child, how can you be so ridiculous ? Why,
he hasn't a bob. He's a perfectly commonplace young man. (*He
turns and crosses* R., *and to above the settee.*) It's so absurd I can't
even be angry with you.

ELIZABETH. I've fallen desperately in love with him, Arnold.

ARNOLD (*turning* R. *of the settee*). Well, you'd better fall desperately out.

ELIZABETH. He wants to marry me.

ARNOLD (*moving down*). I daresay he does. He can go to hell.

ELIZABETH. It's no good talking like that.

ARNOLD (*moving towards* C., *below the settee*). Is he your lover ?

ELIZABETH. No, certainly not.

ARNOLD. It shows that he's a mean skunk to take advantage of my hospitality to make love to you.

ELIZABETH. He's never even kissed me.

ARNOLD (*easing a little* R.). I'd try telling that to the horse marines if I were you.

ELIZABETH (*rising and crossing to* L. *of* ARNOLD). It's because I wanted to do nothing shabby that I told you straight out how things were.

ARNOLD (*turning to her*). How long have you been thinking of this ?

ELIZABETH (*sitting* C. *of the settee*). I've been in love with Teddie ever since I knew him.

ARNOLD (*standing below the* R. *end of the settee*). And you never thought of me at all, I suppose.

ELIZABETH. Oh, yes, I did. (*Turning away.*) I was miserable. But I can't help myself. I wish I loved you, but I don't.

ARNOLD (*crossing* L. *to below the card table*). I recommend you to think very carefully before you do anything foolish.

ELIZABETH. I have thought very carefully.

ARNOLD (*turning*). By God ! I don't know why I don't give you a sound hiding. I'm not sure if that wouldn't be the best thing to bring you to your senses.

ELIZABETH. Oh, Arnold, don't take it like that.

ARNOLD. How do you expect me to take it ? (*Moving to the* L. *end of the settee*.) You come to me quite calmly and say : " I've had enough of you. We've been married three years and I think I'd like to marry somebody else now. Shall I break up your home ? What a bore for you ! Do you mind my divorcing you ? (*Crossing above the settee to* R.) It'll smash up your career, will it ? What a pity ! " (*Crossing down* R.) Oh, no, my girl, I may be a fool, but I'm not a damned fool.

ELIZABETH. Teddie is leaving here by the first train tomorrow. I warn you that I mean to join him as soon as he can make the necessary arrangements.

ARNOLD (*moving a little up stage* R.). Where is he ?

ELIZABETH. I don't know. I suppose he's in his room.

(ARNOLD *crosses* R., *and rings the bell. For a moment he walks up and down the room impatiently.* ELIZABETH *watches him. The* FOOTMAN *enters* L.)

FOOTMAN. Yes, sir.

ARNOLD. Tell Mr. Luton to come here at once.

ELIZABETH. Ask Mr. Luton if he wouldn't mind coming here for a moment, would you ?

(ARNOLD *moves up to the desk and sits.*)

FOOTMAN. Very good, madam.

(*Exit the* FOOTMAN.)

ELIZABETH (*rising and crossing up to* ARNOLD). What are you going to say to him ?

ARNOLD. That's my business.

ELIZABETH. I wouldn't make a scene if I were you.

ARNOLD. I'm not going to make a scene.

(ELIZABETH *crosses up to the french windows, and looks out to* R. *They wait in silence.* ARNOLD *looks at the* L. *doors.*)

Why did you insist on my mother coming here ?

ELIZABETH. It seemed rather absurd to take up the attitude that I should be contaminated by her when . . .

ARNOLD (*interrupting*). When you were proposing to do exactly the same thing. Well, now you've seen her what do you think of her ? Do you think it's been a success ? Is that the sort of woman a man would like his mother to be ?

ELIZABETH. I've been ashamed. I've been so sorry. It all seemed dreadful and horrible. This morning I happened to notice a rose in the garden. It was all overblown and bedraggled. It looked like a painted old woman. And I remembered that I'd looked at it a day or two ago. It was lovely then, fresh and blooming and fragrant. It may be hideous now, but that doesn't take away from the beauty it had once. That was real.

ARNOLD. Poetry, by God ! (*Rising.*) As if this were the moment for poetry ! (*He crosses down to the chair* R. *of the settee.*)

(TEDDIE *comes in* L., *and closes the doors. He has changed into a dinner jacket.*)

TEDDIE (*to* ELIZABETH). Did you want me ?

ARNOLD. *I* sent for you.

(TEDDIE *looks from* ARNOLD *to* ELIZABETH. *He sees that something has happened. He moves to above the card table.*)

When would it be convenient for you to leave this house ?

TEDDIE. I was proposing to go tomorrow morning. But I can very well go at once if you like.

ARNOLD. I do like.

TEDDIE. Very well. Is there anything else you wish to say to me ?

ARNOLD. Do you think it was a very honourable thing to come down here and make love to my wife ?

TEDDIE (*putting his hands in his pockets*). No, I don't. I haven't been very happy about it. That's why I wanted to go away.

ARNOLD. Upon my word you're cool.

TEDDIE.   I'm afraid it's no good saying I'm sorry and that sort of thing. You know what the situation is.

ARNOLD.   Is it true that you want to marry Elizabeth ?

TEDDIE (*taking his hands out of his pockets*). Yes.

(ELIZABETH *moves down a little*.)

I should like to marry her as soon as ever I can.

ARNOLD (*retreating a pace*). Have you thought of me at all ? Has it struck you that you're destroying my home and breaking up my happiness ?

TEDDIE.   I don't see how there could be much happiness for you if Elizabeth doesn't care for you.

ARNOLD (*crossing to* C.). Let me tell you that I refuse to have my home broken up by a twopenny-halfpenny adventurer who takes advantage of a foolish woman.

(ELIZABETH *moves down to the chair* R.)

I refuse to allow myself to be divorced. I can't prevent my wife from going off with you if she's determined to make a damned fool of herself, but this I tell you : nothing will induce me to divorce her.

ELIZABETH.   Arnold, that would be monstrous.

TEDDIE (*with a step towards* ARNOLD). We could force you.

ARNOLD.   How ?

TEDDIE.   If we went away together openly you'd have to bring an action.

(*A slight pause.*)

ARNOLD.   Twenty-four hours after you leave this house I shall go down to Brighton with a chorus girl. And neither you nor I will be able to get a divorce. We've had enough divorces in our family. And now get out, get out, get out ! (*He goes up* C. *to the windows.*)

(TEDDIE *looks uncertainly at* ELIZABETH.)

ELIZABETH (*with a little smile*). Don't bother about me. I shall be all right.

ARNOLD (*at the windows*). Get out ! Get out !

QUICK CURTAIN.

ACT III

The Scene is the same. It is the night of the same day as that on which Act II takes place.

When the curtain rises, CHAMPION-CHENEY *and* ARNOLD, *both in dinner jackets, are on stage.* CHAMPION-CHENEY *is seated at the desk, on which are some illustrated journals. He is looking through the pages of a photograph album.* ARNOLD *is walking restlessly about the room, around* L.C. *The* FOOTMAN *is at the settee table, about to take away the coffee tray. The* BUTLER *is just entering* R. *He moves down* R. *of the settee, and adjusts both cushions. He then adjusts the* L. *chair and moves to the* L. *door and opens it. The* FOOTMAN *moves* L. *with the tray. They both go out, closing the door.* ARNOLD *moves down* L. *CHAMPION-CHENEY rises, the album in his hand.*

C.-C. (*moving to* C., *above the settee table*). I think, if you'll follow my advice to the letter, you'll probably work the trick. (*He puts the album on the settee table.*)

ARNOLD. I don't like it you know. It's against all my principles. (*He sits in the chair* L.)

C.-C. (*moving down to above the* L. *chair*). My dear Arnold, we all hope that you have before you a distinguished political career. You can't learn too soon that the most useful thing about a principle is that it can always be sacrificed to expediency.

ARNOLD. But supposing it doesn't come off? Women are incalculable.

C.-C. (*crossing to below the settee*). Nonsense! A woman will always sacrifice herself if you give her the opportunity. It is her favourite form of self-indulgence. (*He sits on the settee,* C.)

ARNOLD. I never know whether you're a humourist or a cynic, father.

C.-C. I'm neither, my dear boy; I'm merely a very truthful man. But people are so unused to the truth that they're apt to mistake it for a joke or a sneer.

ARNOLD (*irritably, moving to* L. *of the settee*). It seems so unfair that this should happen to me. I don't like it, you know. I'll do anything rather than lose her.

C.-C. Now, all you have to do is to go to Elizabeth and tell her she can have her freedom. Sacrifice yourself all along the line. I know what women are — the moment every obstacle is removed, half the allurement will be gone.

(ARNOLD *turns up, and exits* L.)

(CHAMPION-CHENEY *moves towards* R., *as* LADY KITTY *and* ELIZABETH *enter up* C., *from the garden.* LADY KITTY *is in a gorgeous evening gown. She moves to the desk up* R.)

47

ELIZABETH.   Where is Lord Porteous ?

C.-C.   I think he's in the dining-room, smoking a cigar. (*He opens the dining-room door*, R., *and calls.*)   Hughie ! (*He moves down to above the settee table.*)

(PORTEOUS *enters* R.   *He goes up to the desk.*   LADY KITTY *takes an illustrated paper from the desk, and, with a haughty air and pursed lips, crosses down to the chair* L., *and sits.*   PORTEOUS *picks up another illustrated paper from the desk and crosses down to the chair* R. *of the settee, and sits.   They are not on speaking terms.*)

PORTEOUS (*as he enters — with a grunt*).   Yes ?   Where's Mrs. Shenstone ?

ELIZABETH (*above the settee table*).   Oh, she had a headache. She's gone to bed.

C.-C.   Arnold and I have just been down to my cottage.

ELIZABETH.   I wondered where you'd gone.

C.-C.   I came across an old photograph album this afternoon. I meant to bring it along before dinner, but I forgot, so we went and fetched it.

ELIZABETH.   Oh, do let me see it !   I love old photographs.

(*He gives her the album, and she, sitting down, puts it on her knees and begins to turn over the pages.   He stands over her.*   LADY KITTY *and* PORTEOUS *take surreptitious glances at one another.*)

C.-C.   I thought it might amuse you to see what pretty women looked like five-and-thirty years ago.   That was the day of beautiful women.

ELIZABETH.   Do you think they were more beautiful then than they are now ?

C.-C.   Oh, much.   Now you see lots of pretty little things, but very few beautiful women.

ELIZABETH.   Aren't their clothes funny ?

C.-C. (*pointing to a photograph*).   That's Mrs. Langtry.

ELIZABETH.   She has a lovely nose.

C.-C.   She was the most wonderful thing you ever saw.   Dowagers used to jump on chairs in order to get a good look at her when she came into a drawing-room.   I was riding with her once, and we had to have the gates of the livery stable closed when she was getting on her horse because the crowd was so great.

ELIZABETH.   And who's that ?

C.-C.   Lady Lonsdale.   That's Lady Dudley.

ELIZABETH.   This is an actress, isn't it ?

C.-C.   It is, indeed.   Ellen Terry.   By George ! how I loved that woman !

ELIZABETH (*with a smile*).   Dear Ellen Terry !

C.-C.   That's Bwabs.   I never saw a smarter man in my life. And Oliver Montagu.   Henry Manners with his eye-glass.

ELIZABETH.   Nice-looking, isn't he ?   And this ?

C.-C. That's Mary Anderson. I wish you could have seen her in " A Winter's Tale." Her beauty just took your breath away. And look ! There's Lady Randolph. Bernal Osborne — the wittiest man I ever knew.

ELIZABETH. I think it's too sweet. I love their absurd bustles and those long sleeves.

C.-C. What figures they had !

ELIZABETH. Oh, but aren't they laced in ? How could they bear it ?

C.-C. They didn't play golf then, and nonsense like that, you know. They hunted, in a tall hat and a long black habit, and they were very gracious and charitable to the poor in the village.

ELIZABETH. Did the poor like it ?

C.-C. They had a very thin time if they didn't. When they were in London they drove in the Park every afternoon, and they went to ten-course dinners, where they never met anybody they didn't know. And they had their box at the opera when Patti was singing or Madame Albani.

ELIZABETH. Oh, what a lovely little thing ! Who on earth is that ?

C.-C. That ?

ELIZABETH. She looks so fragile, like a piece of exquisite china, with all those furs on and her face up against her muff, and the snow falling.

C.-C. Yes, there was quite a rage at that time for being taken in an artificial snowstorm.

ELIZABETH. What a sweet smile, so roguish and frank, and debonair ! Oh, I wish I looked like that ! Do tell me who it is !

C.-C. Don't you know ?

ELIZABETH. No.

C.-C. Why — it's Kitty.

ELIZABETH. Lady Kitty ! (*She rises and crosses to* LADY KITTY *with the album.*) Oh, my dear, do look ! It's too ravishing. (*She gives the album to her.*) Why didn't you tell me you looked like that ? Everybody must have been in love with you.

(LADY KITTY *takes the album and looks at it. Then she lets it slip to her lap, and covers her face in her hands. She is crying.* CHAMPION-CHENEY *rises and moves up* L.)

(*In consternation.*) My dear, what's the matter ? Oh, what have I done ? I'm so sorry.

LADY KITTY. Don't, don't talk to me. Leave me alone. It's stupid of me.

(ELIZABETH *looks at her for a moment perplexed, then, turning round, slips her arm in* CHAMPION-CHENEY'S *and leads him up on to the french windows.*)

ELIZABETH (*as they are going, in a whisper*). Did you do that on purpose ?

(*They exit to the garden.*)

(PORTEOUS *rises and goes over to* LADY KITTY. *He puts his hand on her shoulder. They remain thus for a little while.*)

PORTEOUS. I'm afraid I was very rude to you before dinner, Kitty.

LADY KITTY (*taking his hand which is on her shoulder*). It doesn't matter. I'm sure I was very exasperating.

PORTEOUS. I didn't mean what I said, you know.

LADY KITTY. Neither did I.

PORTEOUS. Of course I know that I'd never have been Prime Minister.

LADY KITTY. How can you talk such nonsense, Hughie ? No one would have had a chance if you'd remained in politics.

PORTEOUS. I haven't the character.

LADY KITTY. You have more character than anyone I've ever met.

PORTEOUS. Besides, I don't know that I much wanted to be Prime Minister.

LADY KITTY. Oh, but I should have been so proud of you. Of course you'd have been Prime Minister.

PORTEOUS. I'd have given you India, you know. I think it would have been a very popular appointment.

LADY KITTY. I don't care twopence about India. I'd have been quite content with Western Australia.

PORTEOUS. My dear, you don't think I'd have let you bury yourself in Western Australia ?

LADY KITTY. Or Barbadoes.

PORTEOUS. Never. It sounds like a cure for flat feet. I'd have kept you in London.

(*He tries to pick up the album to look at the photograph of* LADY KITTY. *She puts her hand over it.*)

LADY KITTY. No, don't look.

PORTEOUS (*taking her hand away*). Don't be so silly. (*He takes the book down* C. *of the settee and sits.*)

LADY KITTY. Isn't it hateful to grow old ?

PORTEOUS. You know, you haven't changed much.

LADY KITTY (*enchanted*). Oh, Hughie, how can you talk such nonsense ?

PORTEOUS. Of course you're a little more mature, but that's all. A woman's all the better for being rather mature.

LADY KITTY. Do you really think that ?

PORTEOUS. Upon my soul I do.

LADY KITTY. You're not saying it just to please me ?

PORTEOUS. No, no.

(*A pause.*)

LADY KITTY (*rising, moving to the settee*). Let me look at the photograph again. (*She sits* L. *of* PORTEOUS, *takes the album and looks at the photograph complacently.*) The fact is, if your bones are good, age doesn't really matter. You'll always be beautiful.

PORTEOUS (*with a little smile, almost as if he were talking to a child*). It was silly of you to cry. (*He pats her hand.*)

LADY KITTY. It hasn't made my eyelashes run, has it ?

PORTEOUS. Not a bit.

LADY KITTY. It's very good stuff I use now. They don't stick together, either.

PORTEOUS (*closing the book*). Look here, Kitty, how much longer do you want to stay here ?

LADY KITTY. Oh, I'm quite ready to go whenever you like.

PORTEOUS. Clive gets on my nerves. I don't like the way he keeps hanging about you.

(*A pause. She looks at* PORTEOUS; *surprised, rather amused, and delighted.*)

LADY KITTY. Hughie, you don't mean to say you're jealous of poor Clive ?

PORTEOUS. Of course I'm not jealous of him, but he does look at you in a way that I can't help thinking rather objectionable.

LADY KITTY. Hughie, you may throw me downstairs like Amy Robsart ; you may drag me about the floor by the hair of my head ; I don't care, you're jealous. I shall never grow old.

PORTEOUS. Damn it all, the man was your husband.

LADY KITTY. My dear Hughie, he never had your style. Why, the moment you come into a room everyone looks and says : " Who the devil is that ? "

PORTEOUS. What ? You think that, do you ? Well, I daresay there's something in what you say. These damned Radicals can say what they like, but, by God, Kitty, when a man's a gentleman — well, damn it all, you know what I mean.

LADY KITTY. I think Clive has degenerated dreadfully since we left him.

(PORTEOUS *looks round, then puts his arm round* LADY KITTY.)

PORTEOUS. What do you say to making a bee line for Italy and going to San Michele ?

LADY KITTY. Oh, Hughie ! It's years since we were there.

PORTEOUS. Wouldn't you like to see it — just once more ?

LADY KITTY. Do you remember the first time we went ? It was the most heavenly place I'd ever seen. We'd only left England a month, and I said I'd like to spend all my life there.

PORTEOUS. Of course, I remember. And in a fortnight it was yours, lock, stock and barrel.

LADY KITTY. We were very happy there, Hughie.

PORTEOUS. Let's go back once more.

(*A slight pause.*)

LADY KITTY. I daren't. It must be all peopled with the ghosts of our past. One should never go again to a place where one has been happy. (*Taking his hand.*) It would break my heart.

PORTEOUS. Do you remember how we used to sit on the terrace of the old castle and look at the Adriatic ? We might have been the only people in the world, you and I, Kitty.

(CHAMPION-CHENEY *appears on the terrace, from* L. *of the windows.*)

LADY KITTY (*tragically*). And we thought our love would last for ever.

(*They hear* CHAMPION-CHENEY, *and break apart. Enter* CHAMPION-CHENEY.)

PORTEOUS. Is there any chance of bridge this evening ?

C.-C. (*moving down* R.). I don't think we can make up a four.

PORTEOUS. What a nuisance that boy went away like that ! He wasn't a bad player.

C.-C. Teddie Luton ?

LADY KITTY. I think it was very funny his going without saying good-bye to anyone.

C.-C. (*crossing* L., *above the settee*). The young men of the present day are very casual.

PORTEOUS. I thought there was no train in the evening.

C.-C. There isn't. The last train leaves at 5.45. (*He sits in the chair* L.)

PORTEOUS. How did he go then ?

C.-C. He went.

PORTEOUS. Damned selfish I call it.

LADY KITTY (*intrigued*). Why did he go, Clive ?

(CHAMPION-CHENEY *looks at her for a moment reflectively, leaning forward in his chair.*)

C.-C. I have something very grave to say to you. Elizabeth wants to leave Arnold.

LADY KITTY. Clive ! What on earth for ?

C.-C. She's in love with Teddie Luton. That's why he went. The men of my family are really very unfortunate.

PORTEOUS (*rising*). Does she want to run away with him ?

LADY KITTY (*with consternation*). My dear, what's to be done ?

C.-C. I think you can do a great deal.

LADY KITTY. I ? What ?

C.-C. (*rising, and moving to the* L. *end of the settee*). Tell her, tell her what it means.

(*He looks at her fixedly. She stares at him. A pause.*)

LADY KITTY. Oh, no, no !

C.-C. She's a child. Not for Arnold's sake. For her sake. You must.

(PORTEOUS *moves away a little.*)

LADY KITTY. You don't know what you're asking.

C.-C. Yes, I do.

LADY KITTY. Hughie, what shall I do ?

PORTEOUS (*turning to her*). Do what you like. (*Patting her shoulder.*) I shall never blame you for anything. (*He moves* R.)

(*The* FOOTMAN *comes in* L. *with a letter on a salver. He hesitates on seeing that* ELIZABETH *is not in the room.*)

C.-C. (*turning*). What is it ?

(PORTEOUS *puts the album on the settee table and breaks* R.)

FOOTMAN. I was looking for Mrs. Champion-Cheney, Sir.

C.-C. She's not here. Is that a letter ?

FOOTMAN. Yes, sir. It's just been sent up from the " Champion Arms."

C.-C. I'll give it to Mrs. Cheney.

FOOTMAN. Very good, sir.

(*He brings the tray to* CHAMPION-CHENEY *who takes the letter. The* FOOTMAN *exits* L.)

PORTEOUS. Is the " Champion Arms " the local pub ?

C.-C. (*looking at the letter*). It's by way of being a hotel, but I never heard of anyone staying there.

LADY KITTY. If there was no train I suppose he had to go there.

C.-C. Great minds. I wonder what he has to write about ! (*He goes up to the french windows and calls:*) Elizabeth !

ELIZABETH (*outside*). Yes.

(PORTEOUS *sits in the chair* R. *of the settee.*)

C.-C. Here's a note for you. (*He moves to* L. *of the windows.*)

(*There is silence. They wait for* ELIZABETH *to come. She enters.*)

ELIZABETH. It's lovely in the garden tonight.

C.-C. They've just sent this up from the " Champion Arms." (*Giving her the letter.*)

ELIZABETH. Thank you. (*She crosses to the desk up* R. *and without embarrassment she opens the letter.*)

(CHAMPION-CHENEY *moves* L., *and sits in the chair* L. *of the windows. They all watch* ELIZABETH *as she reads the letter. It covers three pages.* LADY KITTY *becomes impatient. She turns and looks at* CHAMPION-CHENEY, *who nods to her as* ELIZABETH *finishes reading and sits by the desk.*)

LADY KITTY (*turning to* PORTEOUS). Hughie, I wish you'd fetch me a wrap.

(PORTEOUS *rises, and crosses* L.)

I'd like to take a little stroll in the garden, but after thirty years in Italy I find these English summers rather chilly.

(PORTEOUS *turns, smiles at her, and exits* L.)

(ELIZABETH *is lost in thought.*)

I want to talk to Elizabeth, Clive.

C.-C. (*rising*). I'll leave you.

(*He exits* L.)

LADY KITTY. What does he say ?

ELIZABETH. Who ?

LADY KITTY. Mr. Luton.

ELIZABETH (*gives a little start. Then she looks at* LADY KITTY). They've told you ?

LADY KITTY. Yes. And now they have I think I knew it all along.

ELIZABETH (*moving down to* R. *of the settee*). I don't expect you to have much sympathy for me. Arnold is your son.

LADY KITTY. So pitifully little.

ELIZABETH. I'm not suited for this sort of existence. Arnold wants me to take what he calls my place in Society. Oh, I get so bored with those parties in London. All those middle-aged painted women, in beautiful clothes, lolloping round ballrooms with rather old young men. And the endless luncheons where they gossip about so-and-so's love affairs.

LADY KITTY. Are you very much in love with Mr. Luton ?

ELIZABETH (*looking down at the letter*). I love him with all my heart.

LADY KITTY. And he ?

ELIZABETH. He's never cared for anyone but me. He never will.

LADY KITTY. Will Arnold let you divorce him ?

ELIZABETH. No, he won't hear of it. He refuses even to divorce me.

LADY KITTY. Why ?

ELIZABETH. He thinks a scandal will revive all the old gossip.

LADY KITTY. Oh, my poor child !

ELIZABETH. It can't be helped. I'm quite willing to accept the consequences.

LADY KITTY. You don't know what it is to have a man tied to you only by his honour. When married people don't get on they can separate, but if they're not married it's impossible. It's a tie that only death can sever.

ELIZABETH (*moving to below the settee*). If Teddie stopped caring for me I shouldn't want him to stay with me for five minutes.

LADY KITTY. One says that when one's sure of a man's love, but when one isn't any more — oh, it's so different. In those circumstances one's got to keep a man's love. It's the only thing one has.

ELIZABETH. I'm a human being. I can stand on my own feet.

LADY KITTY. Have you any money of your own ?

ELIZABETH. None.

LADY KITTY. Then how can you stand on your own feet ? You think I'm a silly, frivolous woman, but I've learnt something in a bitter school. They can make what laws they like, they can give us the suffrage, but when you come down to bedrock it's the man who pays the piper who calls the tune.

(ELIZABETH *sits* R. *of* LADY KITTY.)

Woman will only be the equal of man when she earns her living in the same way that he does.

ELIZABETH (*smiling*). It sounds rather funny to hear you talk like that.

LADY KITTY. A cook who marries a butler can snap her fingers (*snapping her fingers*) in his face because she can earn just as much as he can. But a woman in your position and a woman in mine will always be dependent on the men who keep them.

ELIZABETH. I don't want luxury. You don't know how sick I am of all this beautiful furniture. These over-decorated houses are like a prison in which I can't breathe. When I drive about in a Callot frock and a Rolls-Royce I envy the shop-girl in a coat and skirt whom I see jumping on the tailboard of a bus.

LADY KITTY. You mean that if need be you could earn your own living ?

ELIZABETH. Yes.

LADY KITTY. What could you be ? A nurse or a typist? It's nonsense. Luxury saps a woman's nerve. And when she's known it once it becomes a necessity.

ELIZABETH. That depends on the woman.

LADY KITTY. When we're young we think we're different from everyone else, but when we grow a little older we discover we're all very much of a muchness.

ELIZABETH (*rising*). You're very kind to take so much trouble about me.

LADY KITTY. It breaks my heart to think that you're going to make the same pitiful mistake that I made.

ELIZABETH (*looking away*). Oh, don't say it was that, don't, don't.

LADY KITTY. Look at me, Elizabeth, and look at Hughie. Do you think it's been a success ? If I had my time over again do you think I'd do it again ? Do you think he would ?

ELIZABETH (*sitting again*). You see, you don't know how much I love Teddie.

LADY KITTY. And do you think I didn't love Hughie ? Do you think he didn't love me ?

ELIZABETH. I'm sure he did.

LADY KITTY. Oh, of course in the beginning it was heavenly. We felt so brave and adventurous and we were so much in love. The first two years were wonderful. People cut me, you know, but I didn't mind. I thought love was everything. It *is* a little uncomfortable when you come upon an old friend and go towards her eagerly, so glad to see her, and are met with an icy stare.

ELIZABETH. Do you think friends like that are worth having ?

LADY KITTY. Perhaps they're not very sure of themselves.
Perhaps they're honestly shocked. It's a test one had better not
put one's friends to if one can help it. It's rather bitter to find
how few one has.

ELIZABETH. But one has some.

LADY KITTY. Yes, they ask you to come and see them when
they're quite certain no one will be there who might object to
meeting you. Or else they say to you : " My dear, you know I'm
devoted to you, and I wouldn't mind at all, (*she pauses*) but my
girl's growing up — I'm sure you understand ; you won't think it
unkind of me if I don't ask you to the house ? "

ELIZABETH (*smiling*). That doesn't seem to me very serious.

LADY KITTY. At first I thought it rather a relief, because it
threw Hughie and me together more. But you know, men are very
funny. Even when they are in love they're not in love all day long.
They want change and recreation.

ELIZABETH. I'm not inclined to blame them for that, poor dears.

LADY KITTY (*easing along the settee nearer to* ELIZABETH). Then
we settled in Florence. And because we couldn't get the society
we'd been used to, we became used to the society we could get.
Loose women and vicious men. Snobs who liked to patronise people
with a handle to their names. And then Hughie began to hanker
after his old life. He wanted to go big game shooting, but I dared
not let him go. I was afraid he'd never come back.

ELIZABETH. But you knew he loved you.

LADY KITTY. Oh, my dear, what a blessed institution marriage
is — for women, and what fools they are to meddle with it ! The
Church is so wise to take its stand on the indi — indi —

ELIZABETH. Solu —

LADY KITTY. Bility of marriage. Believe me, it's no joke when
you have to rely only on yourself to keep a man. I could never
afford to grow old. (*She pauses and looks round.*) My dear . . . I'll
tell you a secret that I've never told a living soul.

ELIZABETH. What is that ?

LADY KITTY. My hair is not naturally this colour.

ELIZABETH. Really.

LADY KITTY. I touch it up. You would never have guessed,
would you ?

ELIZABETH. Never.

LADY KITTY. Nobody does. My dear, it's white, prematurely
of course, but white. I always think it's a symbol of my life. Are
you interested in symbolism ? I think it's too wonderful.

ELIZABETH. I don't think I know very much about it.

LADY KITTY. However tired I've been I've had to be brilliant
and gay. I've never let Hughie see the aching heart behind my
smiling eyes.

ELIZABETH (*amused and touched*). You poor dear.

LADY KITTY. And when I saw he was attracted by someone

else the fear and the jealousy that seized me ! (*She touches* ELIZABETH's *wedding ring.*) You see, I didn't dare make a scene as I should have done if I'd been married — I had to pretend not to notice.

ELIZABETH (*taken aback; drawing her hand away*). But do you mean to say he fell in love with anyone else ?

LADY KITTY. Of course he did — eventually.

ELIZABETH (*hardly knowing what to say*). You must have been very unhappy.

LADY KITTY. Oh, I was, dreadfully. Night after night I sobbed my heart out when Hughie told me he was going to play cards at the club and I knew he was with that — odious woman. Of course, it wasn't as if there weren't plenty of men who were only too anxious to console me. Men have always been attracted by me, you know.

ELIZABETH. Oh, of course, I can quite understand it.

LADY KITTY. But I had my self-respect to think of. I felt that whatever Hughie did I would do nothing that I should regret.

ELIZABETH. You must be very glad now.

LADY KITTY. Oh, yes. Notwithstanding all my temptations I've been absolutely faithful to Hughie in spirit.

ELIZABETH. I don't think I quite understand what you mean.

LADY KITTY. Well, there was a poor Italian boy, young Count Castel Giovanni, who was so desperately in love with me that his mother begged me not to be too cruel. She was afraid he'd go into a consumption. What could I do ? And then, oh, years later, there was Antonio Melita. He said he'd shoot himself unless I — well, you understand I couldn't let the poor boy shoot himself.

ELIZABETH. D'you think he really would have shot himself ?

LADY KITTY. Oh, one never knows, you know. Those Italians are so passionate. He was really rather a lamb. He had such beautiful eyes.

(ELIZABETH *looks at her for a long time and a certain horror seizes her of this dissolute painted old woman.*)

ELIZABETH (*hoarsely, turning away*). Oh, but I think that's — dreadful.

LADY KITTY. Are you shocked ? One sacrifices one's life for love and then one finds that love doesn't last. The tragedy of love isn't death or separation. One gets over them. The tragedy of love is indifference.

(ARNOLD *enters* L.)

ARNOLD. Excuse me — may I have a little talk with you, Elizabeth ?

ELIZABETH. Of course.

ARNOLD. Shall we go into another room ?

ELIZABETH. If you like.

LADY KITTY (*rising*). No, stay here. (*She moves* L.) I'm going out anyway.

E

(*Exit* LADY KITTY L.)

ARNOLD (*moving towards* ELIZABETH). I want you to listen to me for a few minutes, Elizabeth. I was so taken aback by what you told me just now that I lost my head. I was rather absurd and I beg your pardon. I said things I regret.

ELIZABETH. Oh, don't blame yourself. I'm sorry that I should have given you occasion to say them.

ARNOLD. I want to ask you if you've quite made up your mind to go.

ELIZABETH. Quite.

ARNOLD. Just now I seem to have said all that I didn't want to say and nothing that I did. I'm stupid and tongue-tied : I never told you how deeply I loved you.

ELIZABETH. Oh, Arnold !

ARNOLD. Please let me speak now. It's so very difficult. If I seemed absorbed in politics and the house, and so on, to the exclusion of my interest in you, I'm dreadfully sorry. I suppose it was absurd of me to think you would take my great love for granted.

ELIZABETH. But, Arnold, I'm not reproaching you.

ARNOLD. I'm reproaching myself. (*Sitting on her left.*) I've been tactless and neglectful. But I do ask you to believe that it hasn't been because I didn't love you. Can you forgive me ?

ELIZABETH. I don't think that there's anything to forgive.

ARNOLD. It wasn't till today when you talked of leaving me that I realised how desperately in love with you I was.

ELIZABETH (*rising*). After three years ? (*She crosses to* R. *of the settee.*)

ARNOLD. I'm so proud of you. I admire you so much. When I see you at a party, so fresh and lovely, and everybody wondering at you, I have a sort of little thrill to think you're mine, and afterwards I shall take you home.

ELIZABETH (*turning to him*). Oh, Arnold, you're exaggerating.

ARNOLD. I can't imagine this house without you. Life seems on a sudden all empty and meaningless. (*He rises.*) Oh, Elizabeth, don't you love me at all ?

ELIZABETH. It's much better to be honest. No.

ARNOLD. Doesn't my love mean anything to you ?

ELIZABETH. I'm very grateful to you. I'm sorry to cause you pain. What would be the good of my staying with you when I should be wretched all the time ?

ARNOLD. Do you love that man as much as all that ? (*Not looking at her.*) Does my unhappiness mean nothing to you ?

ELIZABETH. Of course it does. It breaks my heart. (*She takes a step towards him.*) You see, I never knew I meant so much to you. I'm so touched. And I'm so sorry, Arnold, really sorry. But I can't help myself.

ARNOLD. Poor child, it's cruel of me to torture you.

ELIZABETH (*taking another step towards him*). Oh, Arnold, believe me, I have tried to make the best of it. (*Sitting on the settee,* R. *end.*) I've tried to love you, but I can't. After all, one either loves or one doesn't. Trying is no help. And now I'm at the end of my tether. I can't help the consequences — I must do what my whole self yearns for.

ARNOLD (L. *of the settee*). My poor child, I'm so afraid you'll be unhappy. I'm so afraid you'll regret.

ELIZABETH. You must leave me to my fate. (*Turning her head away.*) I hope you'll forget me and all the unhappiness I've caused you.

(*There is a pause.* ARNOLD *moves up* C., *and down again reflectively. Then he stops and faces her.*)

ARNOLD. If you love this man and want to go to him I'll do nothing to prevent you. My only wish is to do what is best for you.

ELIZABETH (*facing him*). Arnold, that's awfully kind of you. If I'm treating you badly at least I want you to know that I'm grateful for all your kindness to me.

ARNOLD. But there's one favour I should like you to do me. Will you ?

ELIZABETH. Oh, Arnold, of course I'll do anything I can.

ARNOLD (*sitting on her* L.). Luton hasn't very much money. You've been used to a certain amount of luxury, and I can't bear to think that you should do without anything you've had. It would kill me to think that you were suffering any hardship or privation.

ELIZABETH. Oh, but Teddie can earn enough for our needs. After all, we don't want much money.

ARNOLD. I'm afraid my mother's life hasn't been very easy, but it's obvious that the only thing that's made it possible is that Porteous was rich. I want you to let me make you an allowance of two thousand a year.

ELIZABETH. Oh, no, I couldn't think of it. It's absurd.

ARNOLD. I beg you to accept it. You don't know what a difference it will make.

ELIZABETH. It's awfully kind of you, Arnold. It humiliates me to speak about it. Nothing would induce me to take a penny from you.

ARNOLD. Well, you can't prevent me from opening an account at my bank in your name. The money *shall* be paid in every quarter whether you touch it or not, and if you happen to want it, it will be there waiting for you.

ELIZABETH. You overwhelm me, Arnold. There's only one thing I· want you to do for me. I should be very grateful if you would divorce me as soon as you possibly can.

ARNOLD. No, I won't do that. But I'll give you cause to divorce me.

ELIZABETH. You !

ARNOLD. Yes. But of course you'll have to be very careful for a bit. I'll put it through as quickly as possible, but I'm afraid you can't hope to be free for over six months.

ELIZABETH. But, Arnold, your seat and your political career !

ARNOLD (*rising*). Oh, well, my father gave up his seat under similar circumstances. (*He picks up the album and crosses* L., *and up to the settee table.*) He's got along very comfortably without politics.

ELIZABETH. But they're your whole life.

ARNOLD. After all one can't have it both ways. You can't serve God and Mammon. If you want to do the decent thing you have to be prepared to suffer for it.

ELIZABETH. But I don't want you to suffer for it.

ARNOLD. At first I rather hesitated at the scandal. But I daresay that was only weakness on my part. Under the circumstances I should have liked to keep out of the Divorce Court if I could.

ELIZABETH (*turning away*). Arnold, you're making me absolutely miserable.

(*There is a pause.*)

ARNOLD (*moving down,* L. *of the settee*). What you said before dinner was quite right. It's nothing for a man, but it makes so much difference to a woman. Naturally I must think of you first.

ELIZABETH. That's absurd. (*Rising.*) It's out of the question. (*Moving towards* ARNOLD.) Whatever there's to pay I must pay it.

ARNOLD. It's not very much I'm asking you, Elizabeth.

ELIZABETH. I'm taking everything from you.

ARNOLD. It's the only condition I make. My mind is absolutely made up. I will never divorce you, but I will enable you to divorce me.

ELIZABETH (*turning away*). Oh, Arnold, it's cruel to be so generous.

ARNOLD. It's not generous at all. It's the only way I have of showing you how deep and passionate and sincere my love is for you.

(*There is a silence.* ELIZABETH *turns to him. He holds out his hand.*)

Goodnight. I have a great deal of work to do before I go to bed.

ELIZABETH (*taking his hand*). Goodnight.

ARNOLD. Do you mind if I kiss you ?

ELIZABETH (*with agony*). Oh, Arnold !

(*He gravely kisses her on the forehead and then goes out* L. ELIZABETH *stands lost in thought. Then she sits at the* L. *end of the settee. She is shattered.* LADY KITTY *and* PORTEOUS *come in at the windows.* LADY KITTY *wears a wrap.* PORTEOUS *is on her* R.)

LADY KITTY (*moving down*). You're alone, Elizabeth ?

ELIZABETH (*rising and moving up* L.). That note you asked me about, Lady Kitty, from Teddie . . .

LADY KITTY. Yes ?

ELIZABETH. He wanted to have a talk with me before he went away. He's waiting for me in the summer house by the tennis court. Would Lord Porteous mind going down and asking him to come here ?

PORTEOUS. Certainly. Certainly.

ELIZABETH. Forgive me for troubling you. But it's very important.

PORTEOUS. No trouble at all.

(*He exits at the french windows, to* R.)

LADY KITTY (*moving as if about to go*). Hughie and I will leave you alone.

ELIZABETH. But I don't want to be left alone. I want you to stay.

(*A pause.* LADY KITTY *brings* ELIZABETH *down to* R. *of the settee.*)

LADY KITTY. What are you going to say to him ?

ELIZABETH (*desperately*). Please don't ask me questions. I'm so frightfully unhappy. (*She sits in the chair* R. *of the settee.*)

LADY KITTY (*moving towards her*). My poor child !

ELIZABETH. Oh, isn't life rotten ? Why can't one be happy without making other people unhappy ?

LADY KITTY. I wish I knew how to help you. I'm simply devoted to you. (*She hunts about in her mind for something to do or say, then fiddles in her handbag.*) Would you like my lipstick ?

ELIZABETH (*smiling through her tears*). Thanks. I never use one.

LADY KITTY. Oh, but just try. It's such a comfort when you're in trouble.

(*Enter* PORTEOUS *and* TEDDIE *up* C.)

PORTEOUS. I brought him. He said he'd be damned if he'd come.

LADY KITTY (*moving up to below and* L. *of* TEDDIE). When a lady sent for him ? Are these the manners of the young men of today ?

(PORTEOUS *moves to up* L.C.)

TEDDIE (*easing towards* LADY KITTY). When you've been solemnly kicked out of a house once I think it seems rather pushing to come back again as though nothing had happened.

ELIZABETH. Teddie, I want you to be serious.

TEDDIE (*moving down* R. *of the settee*). Darling, I had such a rotten dinner at that pub. If you ask me to be serious on the top of that I shall cry.

ELIZABETH. Don't be idiotic, Teddie. (*Her voice faltering.*) I'm so utterly wretched.

(TEDDIE *looks at her for a moment gravely.* LADY KITTY *turns to* PORTEOUS, *who helps her take off her wrap.*)

TEDDIE. What is it ?

ELIZABETH. I can't come away with you, Teddie.

TEDDIE. Why not ?

ELIZABETH (*looking away in embarrassment*). I don't love you enough.

TEDDIE. Fiddle !

ELIZABETH (*with a flash of anger*). Don't say " Fiddle " to me.

TEDDIE. I shall say exactly what I like to you.

ELIZABETH. I won't be bullied.

TEDDIE. Now look here, Elizabeth, you know perfectly well that I'm in love with you, and I know perfectly well that you're in love with me. So what are you talking nonsense for ?

ELIZABETH (*her voice breaking*). I can't say it if you're cross with me.

TEDDIE (*kneeling by her and smiling very tenderly*). I'm not cross with you, silly.

ELIZABETH. It's harder still when you're being rather an owl.

TEDDIE (*with a chuckle*). Am I mistaken in thinking you're not very easy to please ?

ELIZABETH. Oh, it's monstrous. I was all wrought up and ready to do anything, and now you've thoroughly put me out. I feel like a great big fat balloon that someone has put a long pin into. (*With a sudden look at him.*) Have you done it on purpose ?

TEDDIE (*rising*). Upon my soul I don't know what you're talking about.

ELIZABETH. I wonder if you're really much cleverer than I think you are.

TEDDIE (*taking her hands and pulling her up*). Now tell me exactly what you want to say. By the way, do you want Lady Kitty and Lord Porteous to be here ?

ELIZABETH. Yes.

LADY KITTY (*moving down* L. *to below the settee*). Elizabeth asked us to stay.

TEDDIE. Oh, I don't mind, bless you. I only thought you might feel rather in the way.

LADY KITTY (*frigidly*). A gentlewoman never feels in the way, Mr. Luton. (*She sits on the settee, at the* L. *end.*)

TEDDIE. Won't you call me Teddie ? Everybody does, you know.

(LADY KITTY *tries to give him a withering look, but she finds it very difficult to prevent herself from smiling.* TEDDIE *strokes* ELIZABETH's *hands. She draws them away.*)

ELIZABETH (*by the chair* R. *of the settee*). No, don't do that. Teddie, it wasn't true when I said I didn't love you. Of course I love you. But Arnold loves me, too. I didn't know how much.

TEDDIE (*sitting* R. *of* LADY KITTY). What has he been saying to you ?

(PORTEOUS *moves a little* R., *above the settee.*)

ELIZABETH. He's been very good to me, and so kind. I didn't know he could be so kind. He offered to let me divorce him.

(PORTEOUS *stops.*)

TEDDIE. That's very decent of him.

(PORTEOUS *eases* R. *again.*)

ELIZABETH. But don't you see, it ties my hands. How can I accept such a sacrifice ? I should never forgive myself if I profited by his generosity.

(PORTEOUS *stops.*)

TEDDIE. If another man and I were devilish hungry and there was only one mutton chop between us, and he said, " You eat it," I wouldn't waste a lot of time arguing. I'd wolf it before he changed his mind.

(PORTEOUS *goes to the chair down* R.)

ELIZABETH (*to* R. *of the settee*). Don't talk like that. It maddens me. I'm trying to do the right thing. (*She sits* R. *of* TEDDIE.)

TEDDIE. You're not in love with Arnold ; you're in love with me. It's idiotic to sacrifice your life for a slushy sentiment.

ELIZABETH. After all, I did marry him.

(PORTEOUS *sits down* R.)

TEDDIE. Well, you made a mistake. A marriage without love is no marriage at all.

ELIZABETH. I made the mistake. Why should he suffer for it ? If anyone has to suffer it's only right that I should.

TEDDIE. What sort of a life do you think it would be with him ? When two people are married it's very difficult for one of them to be unhappy without making the other unhappy too.

ELIZABETH. I can't take advantage of his generousity.

TEDDIE. I daresay he'll get a lot of satisfaction out of it.

ELIZABETH. You're being beastly, Teddie. He was simply wonderful. I never knew he had it in him. He was really noble.

TEDDIE (*rising*). You are talking rot, Elizabeth. (*He moves up* R. *of the settee to above it.*)

ELIZABETH. I wonder if you'd be capable of acting like that.

TEDDIE (*turning*). Acting like what ?

ELIZABETH. What would you do if I were married to you and came and told you I loved somebody else and wanted to leave you ?

TEDDIE (*moving down to below the* R. *end of the settee*). You have very pretty blue eyes, Elizabeth. I'd black first one and then the other. And after that we'd see.

ELIZABETH. You damned brute !

TEDDIE (*pushing* ELIZABETH *along the settee, and sitting on her* R.). I've often thought I wasn't quite a gentleman. Had it ever struck you ?

(*They look at one another for a while.*)

ELIZABETH. You know, you are taking an unfair advantage of me. I feel as if I came to you quite unsuspectingly and when I wasn't looking you kicked me on the shins.

TEDDIE.　Don't you think we'd get on rather well together ?

(*A slight pause.*)

PORTEOUS.　Elizabeth's a fool if she don't stick to her husband. It's bad enough for the man, but for the woman — it's damnable. I hold no brief for Arnold.　He plays bridge like a fool.　Saving your presence, Kitty, I think he's a prig.

LADY KITTY.　Poor dear, his father was at his age.　I daresay he'll grow out of it.

PORTEOUS.　But you stick to him, Elizabeth, stick to him.

(TEDDIE *rises and turns to* PORTEOUS.)

Man is a gregarious animal.　We're members of a herd.　If we break the herd's laws we suffer for it.　And we suffer damnably.

(TEDDIE *goes up stage in despair.*)

LADY KITTY (*taking* ELIZABETH'*s hand*).　Oh, Elizabeth, my dear child, don't go.　It's not worth it.　It's not worth it.　I tell you that, and I've sacrificed everything to love.

(*A pause.* TEDDIE *crosses above the settee and down to above the*
L. *chair.*)

ELIZABETH.　I'm afraid.

TEDDIE (*in a whisper*).　Elizabeth.

ELIZABETH (*rising*).　I can't face it. (*Crossing to* TEDDIE.) It's asking too much of me.　Let's say good-bye to one another, Teddie. (*She pauses.*)　It's the only thing to do.　And have pity on me. (*Sitting in the chair* L.)　I'm giving up all my hope of happiness.

TEDDIE (*moving to* R. *of her chair, and looking at her*).　But I wasn't offering you happiness.　I don't think my sort of love tends to happiness.　I'm jealous.　I'm not a very easy man to get on with. I'm often out of temper and irritable.　I should be fed to the teeth with you sometimes, and so would you be with me.　I daresay we'd fight like cat and dog, and sometimes we'd hate each other.　Often you'd be wretched and bored stiff and lonely, and often you'd be frightfully homesick, and then you'd regret all you'd lost.　Stupid women would be rude to you because we'd run away together. And some of them would cut you.　I don't offer you peace and quietness.　I offer you unrest and anxiety.

(ELIZABETH *begins to rise.*)

I don't offer you happiness.　I offer you love.

ELIZABETH (*rising and stretching out her arms*).　You hateful creature, I absolutely adore you !

(TEDDIE *throws his arms round her and kisses her passionately
on the lips.*)

LADY KITTY (*easing along the settee towards the* R. *end*).　Of course the moment he said he'd give her a black eye I knew it was finished.

PORTEOUS (*good-humouredly*). You are a fool, Kitty.

LADY KITTY. I know I am, but I can't help it.

TEDDIE. Let's make a bolt for it now.

ELIZABETH. Shall we ?

TEDDIE. This minute.

(*They move up* C.)

PORTEOUS. You're damned fools, both of you, damned fools !

(TEDDIE *and* ELIZABETH *stop and turn*.)

If you like you can have my car.

TEDDIE (*moving down* R.C., *with* ELIZABETH). That's awfully kind
of you. As a matter of fact I got it out of the garage. It's just
along the drive.

PORTEOUS (*indignantly*). How do you mean, you got it out of
the garage ?

TEDDIE. Well, I thought there'd be a lot of bother, and it
seemed to me the best thing would be for Elizabeth and me not to
stand upon the order of our going, you know. Do it now. (*He
turns to* ELIZABETH. *They both laugh*.) An excellent motto for
a business man.

PORTEOUS. Do you mean to say you were going to steal my car ?

TEDDIE (*to* PORTEOUS). Not exactly. I was only going to
commandeer it, so to speak.

PORTEOUS. I'm speechless. I'm absolutely speechless. (*False
teeth business*.)

TEDDIE. Hang it all, I couldn't carry Elizabeth all the way to
London. (*Turning to* ELIZABETH, *putting his arm round her*.) She's
so damned plump.

ELIZABETH. You dirty dog !

(*They kiss*.)

PORTEOUS (*spluttering*). Well, well, well ! . . . (*Helplessly*.) I like
him, Kitty, it's no good pretending I don't. I like him.

TEDDIE (*looking at the windows*). The moon's shining, Elizabeth.
We'll drive all through the night.

PORTEOUS. They'd better go to San Michele. I'll wire to have it
got ready for them.

LADY KITTY (*rising*). That's where we went when Hughie and
I . . . (*Faltering*.) Oh, you dear things, how I envy you ! (*She
moves away* L., *and a little up stage*.)

PORTEOUS (*mopping his eyes*). Now don't cry, Kitty. Confound
you, don't cry.

TEDDIE (*moving up*). Come, darling.

ELIZABETH (*following him*). But I can't go like this.

TEDDIE. Nonsense ! (*Crossing to* LADY KITTY.) Lady Kitty
will lend you her wrap. Won't you ?

LADY KITTY (*picking up the wrap*). You're capable of tearing it off my back if I don't. (*She crosses to* ELIZABETH *and puts the wrap on her.*)

TEDDIE. And we'll buy you a toothbrush in London in the morning.

LADY KITTY. She must write a note for Arnold. I'll put it on her pincushion.

TEDDIE. Pincushion be blowed ! Come, darling. We'll drive through the dawn and through the sunrise.

ELIZABETH. Good-bye. Good-bye.

(*She kisses* LADY KITTY. TEDDIE *crosses down to* PORTEOUS *and shakes hands, then crosses up to* LADY KITTY *and kisses her. Then, taking* ELIZABETH'*s hand, he goes out with her through the french windows, and off, to* L.)

LADY KITTY. Oh, Hughie, how it all comes back to me ! Will they suffer all we suffered ? And have we suffered all in vain ?

PORTEOUS. My dear, I don't know that in life it matters so much what you do as what you are. (*He puts his arm round her and brings her to the settee.*) No one can learn by the experience of another because no circumstances are quite the same. (*They sit,* LADY KITTY C., *and* PORTEOUS *on her* R.) If we made rather a hash of things perhaps it was because we were rather trivial people. You can do anything in this world if you're prepared to take the consequences, and consequences depend on character.

(*Enter* CHAMPION-CHENEY, L., *rubbing his hands. He is as pleased as Punch.*)

C.-C. Well, I think I've settled the hash of that young man.

LADY KITTY. Oh !

C.-C. (*moving down to* L. *of the settee*). You have to get up very early in the morning to get the better of your humble servant.

(*There is the sound of a car starting.*)

LADY KITTY. What's that noise ?

C.-C. (*moving up stage*). It sounds like a car. (*He pauses, then moves down again.*) I expect it's your chauffeur taking one of the maids for a run.

PORTEOUS. Whose hash are you talking about ?

C.-C. (*sitting on the settee, at the* L. *end*). Mr. Edward Luton's, my dear Hughie. I told Arnold exactly what to do and he's done it. What makes a prison ? Why, bars and bolts. Remove them and a prisoner won't want to escape. Clever, I flatter myself.

PORTEOUS. You were always that, Clive, but at the moment you're obscure.

C.-C.   I told Arnold to go to Elizabeth and tell her she could have her freedom. I told him to sacrifice himself all along the line.

LADY KITTY.   Arnold did that ?

C.-C.   He followed my instructions to the letter. I've just seen him. She's shaken. I'm willing to bet five hundred pounds to a penny that she won't bolt. A downy old bird, eh ? Downy's the word. Downy.

(*He begins to laugh. Then* PORTEOUS *laughs, and then* LADY KITTY. *They are all three in fits of laughter, as*

THE CURTAIN FALLS.

FURNITURE AND PROPERTY PLOT

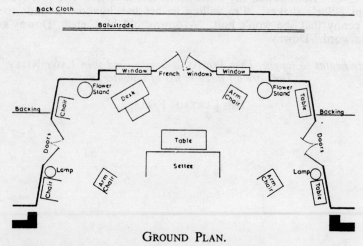

GROUND PLAN.

Carpet on stage.   Curtains at windows as desired.
On the walls:—

Pictures and electric wall brackets.   (*See the photograph of the setting.*)

1 large settee, with cushions (*down* C.).

1 Sheraton chair (R. *of the settee*).

1 Armchair (L. *of the settee*).

1 Chair (*down* R., *below the door*).

1 Chair to match the above (R. *above the* R. *door*).

1 Armchair (*up* L., *near the window*).

2 Flower stands (*up* R., *and up* L.).

1 Carved side table (*up* L., *above the doors*).

1 ditto (L. *below the doors*).

On the above:—Tall vases, as in photograph.

1 Writing desk (*up* R.C., *near the windows*).

On it:—Blotter, inkstand, desk calendar, ashtray, two framed photographs.

2 Tall ornamental floor lamp standards with candelabra (*as in the photograph*).

1 Small table (C. *above the settee*).

On it:—Bowl of flowers, ashtray.

Card table and two chairs for Act II (*ready off stage* L.).

Bell-push in R. wall above the doors.

68

PROPERTIES

ACT I

Personal:—

TEDDIE. 2 Tennis rackets. Cigarette case. Lighter.

CHAMPION-CHENEY (*second entrance*). Lipstick in container.

LADY KITTY. Handbag with usual contents.

ACT II

Stage:—

Playing cards. Bridge scoring book and pencil (*settee table*).

Low coffee stool, and tray of tea things for two persons, including plate of bread and butter, and cakes (*ready off* L. *for the* BUTLER *and* FOOTMAN).

Personal:—

ARNOLD. Large book of furniture illustrations.

TEDDIE. Cigarette case, filled, and lighter.

ACT III

Stage:—

Tray of coffee cups (*on the settee table*, C.).

Three or four illustrated journals (" Tatler," etc.). (*On the writing desk.*)

Personal:—

CHAMPION-CHENEY. Photograph album.

FOOTMAN. Letter in envelope, on a salver (*ready off* L.).

LIGHTING PLOT

ACT I

FLOATS. Straw and pink, at three-quarters.

BATTENS. Straw and pink, full. White, half.

BATTEN SPOTS (*on acting areas* C., R.C., *and* L.C.). No. 36 pink and white (frost) mingled.

BATTEN OVER EXTERIOR. Straw and white, full.

FLOOD ON CLOTH. Straw and white, full.

INTERIOR BACKINGS. Straw lengths.

> No Cues.

ACT II

FLOATS. Straw and pink, at half.

BATTENS. Straw and pink, at three-quarters.

BATTEN SPOTS (*on acting areas*). No. 51 gold (frost).

BATTEN OVER EXTERIOR. Straw (frost).

FLOOD ON CLOTH. Straw (frost).

INTERIOR BACKINGS. Straw lengths.

> No Cues.

ACT III

WALL BRACKETS AND STANDARDS. ON

FLOATS. Straw, pink, and blue, at half.

BATTENS. Straw, pink, and blue, at three-quarters.

BATTEN SPOTS (*on acting areas*). No. 51 gold.

BATTEN OVER EXTERIOR. Amber, and blue, full.

FLOOD ON CLOTH (*to open*). No. 4 amber, and No. 18 blue.

> NOTE.—*As the Act draws to a close, the amber in batten on the exterior and the flood on cloth fade slowly to NIL and No. 20 blue flood is brought in to mingle with the No. 18 floods.*

INTERIOR BACKINGS. No. 4 amber lengths, or flood No. 51 gold.

> No Cues (*apart from the above note*).

MADE AND PRINTED IN GREAT BRITAIN BY
WHITSTABLE LITHO, STRAKER BROTHERS LTD.